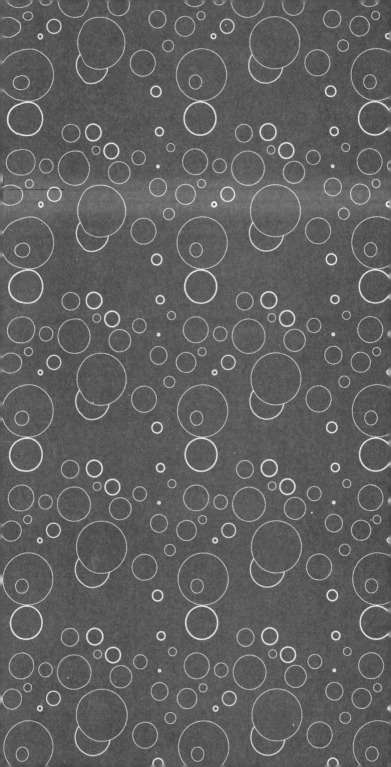

ALCOHOLICA Esoterica

A COLLECTION OF
USEFUL AND USELESS
INFORMATION AS IT
RELATES TO THE
HISTORY AND
CONSUMPTION OF
ALL MANNER OF
BOOZE.

■

IAN LENDLER

PENGUIN BOOKS

P E N G U I N   B O O K S
Published by the Penguin Group
Penguin Group (USA) Inc., 375 Hudson Street,
New York, New York 10014, U.S.A.
Penguin Group (Canada), 90 Eglinton Avenue East, Suite 700,
Toronto, Ontario, Canada M4P 2Y3
(a division of Pearson Penguin Canada Inc.)
Penguin Books Ltd, 80 Strand, London WC2R 0RL, England
Penguin Ireland, 25 St Stephen's Green, Dublin 2, Ireland
(a division of Penguin Books Ltd)
Penguin Group (Australia), 250 Camberwell Road,
Camberwell, Victoria 3124, Australia
(a division of Pearson Australia Group Pty Ltd)
Penguin Books India Pvt Ltd, 11 Community Centre,
Panchsheel Park, New Delhi–110 017, India
Penguin Group (NZ), cnr Airborne and Rosedale Roads,
Albany, Auckland 1310, New Zealand
(a division of Pearson New Zealand Ltd)
Penguin Books (South Africa) (Pty) Ltd, 24 Sturdee Avenue,
Rosebank, Johannesburg 2196, South Africa

Penguin Books Ltd, Registered Offices:
80 Strand, London WC2R 0RL, England

First published in Penguin Books 2005

1   3   5   7   9   10   8   6   4   2

Copyright © Ian Lendler, 2005
All rights reserved

ISBN 0-14-303597-5
CIP DATA AVAILABLE

Printed in the United States of America
Set in New Baskerville with ATSackers, Rubens, and Glorietta
Designed by Sabrina Bowers

To Kusum

For a variety of reasons related to the writing of this book, and having only a little bit to do with the consumption of its subject matter.

ACKNOWLEDGMENTS

First and foremost, I need to thank Tanya McKinnon, who was very, very responsible for my writing this in the first place (as she's always reminding me).

Writing about alcohol is a lot like drinking alcohol. It's much more fun and interesting when you do it with friends. Everyone, and I mean everyone, has managed to acquire snippets of barroom/alcohol trivia in their time. Some of which even turned out to be true. So for putting me onto the scent of various facts in this book, I have to thank: David Goodearl and Howard Smith for remembering all the good bits from history, Marc Lendler, David Cashion, Anthony Crupi, Kevin Doyle, Cullen Duffy, Jason Eaton, Lucy Gadd, Keith Horan, Sami and Tanya Lahdelma, Devin Macintyre, Ray and Lydia Markoff, Pat Robinson, Steve Smith, Sarah Weiss, and finally, the bartenders at 11th St. Bar in Manhattan, who served me alcohol and anecdotes for many fine years.

CONTENTS

WARNING

There is a grave danger that you must be made aware of before reading this book.

You will turn into Cliff Clavin. It happened to me. While writing and researching this book, I learned tons of interesting anecdotes and facts. Within days, I was the nightmare of every party. Like Cliff from *Cheers,* I began peppering every conversation with alcohol-related arcana, and just generally giving the impression that I was losing my grip on the great big world that existed beyond the rim of my pint glass. Very quickly, friends started asking how things were going at home, and slipping me the cards of counselors "who could help."

So, please, only read this book in small doses, *and at all times* with a stiff drink in hand. This will ensure that whatever you read won't be recalled the next day with any real clarity. Your friends and local bartender will thank you for it.

INTRODUCTION

"One must be drunk. . . . If you would not feel the horrible burden of Time that breaks your shoulders and bows you to the earth, you must intoxicate yourself unceasingly. But with what? With wine, with poetry, or with virtue, your choice. But intoxicate yourself." —CHARLES BAUDELAIRE, NINETEENTH-CENTURY FRENCH POET

"What contemptible scoundrel stole the cork from my lunch?" —W.C. FIELDS

In the beginning, there was a grape.

And then a winged insect came, accidentally carrying some yeast that was stuck to its body. And the yeast got on the grape, and also on his grape neighbors. And they fermented in the sun.

A couple of days later, a bird in search of food came along and ate that grape.

And it was *awfully* refreshing, so the bird ate another one. Then another. And soon, the bird started feeling pretty good about his life . . . pretty *darn* good, actually. After all, here he was, eating grapes on a warm, sunny afternoon and, what the heck, it was prehistoric times, so it's not like he had anything *else* to do that day.

So he called his bird friends over to try these new grapes, and soon enough, *they* were all full of good cheer, too, squawking and doing stunt cartwheels in the sky to impress some of the female birds who, having had a few too many grapes of their own, began flashing their plumage.

And ancient man saw this. And he saw that it was good.

According to scientists, this is the best explanation for how mankind first discovered alcohol. After a while, some enterprising human figured out how to harness the grape and create alcohol on purpose. Then, we were off to the races.

The first historical evidence of alcohol is a jug of wine found in the mountains of present-day Iran that dates back to 5400 B.C. The earliest sample of writing ever found is a Sumerian clay tablet that refers to beer in 3300 B.C.

In fact, the history of drinking is an alternate history of the world. Every advance in civilization has been accompanied by a step forward in mixology. Agriculture gave us vineyards, copper gave us distilling, coal furnaces gave us glass bottles, and rubber hosing gave us beer bongs.

Like it or not, certain things like war, god, love, and liquor seem to be intrinsic to human nature. Drinking is a universal language, an international common culture. Whether you're in a chichi bar in Paris or a honky-tonk in Texas, you can fall into a friendly debate with total strangers over the merits of lager versus stout, Scotch versus bourbon, or the drinking world's greatest unending controversy—the proper way to mix a martini.

The reason for this is simple—from the relaxing first drink to the regrettable last drink to the hangover the next day, this ritual has been going on for thousands of years. Along the way, it's been the catalyst for camaraderie, good times, and karaoke, not to mention stupidity, senseless violence, and karaoke.

In other words, as cultures go, drinking's pretty darn interesting.

The problem is, you wouldn't know it if you went

looking around your local bookstore. There are plenty of in-depth books about alcohol, but they tend to be written by and for connoisseurs, people who share more in common with skid-row gutter bums than they'd care to admit. Namely, both groups take their tipple *way* too seriously.

In reality, there are very, very few wine, beer, or whiskey snobs in the world, but there are very, very many people who like to have a few drinks and swap funny stories with friends.

That's where this book comes in. Besides being a general history of and guide to drinking, its main purpose is to serve as a compilation of the best drinking stories from some of the most famous people and events in history. The sort of stories you can swap with friends over drinks on a lazy afternoon.

So if you're interested in debating the molecular differences between French vineyard soil and Italian soil (which I'm not), then you can go to a bookstore and pick up a serious tome by a wine expert (which I'm also not).

But if you want to learn that the sailors on the *Mayflower* forced the Pilgrims out onto Plymouth Rock because they didn't want to sail any farther and risk running out of beer on the return trip to England (true story), then this is definitely the book you should be reading.

This is also the book to read if you want to find out that, statistically speaking, you have a higher chance of being killed by a flying champagne cork than by a poisonous spider, or that the Manhattan cocktail was invented by Winston Churchill's mom.

While not every drink can have as grand a lineage as the Manhattan, each has its own unique story. For instance, whiskey is a tough-guy drink, right? But why? Why don't cowboys in movies mosey into a saloon, slap their dusty saddles on the counter, and ask the barkeep for a drop of sherry?

And why do CEOs celebrate business deals with a bottle of champagne and not a forty-ounce of Colt

.45? Let's be honest, they're all just flavored alcohol. They'll all get you drunk. So how does each drink gain its reputation?

Appreciating the history of a drink is one thing, but appreciating the drink itself can take years of sampling and learned study. Something I have no patience for. To save you the effort, I've boiled down the essential advice from experts to enable you to buy and pour your drink with confidence.

So if you're a beginner, hopefully this book will serve as a travel guide to the land of drinking, describing the beverages you'll encounter along your journey and the pioneers who have gone before you.

If you're a casual imbiber, then you've already settled on a few favorites. I've included enough useful trivia to help you enjoy your particular tipple a bit better, and enough useless trivia to help you kill a few pleasant hours in a bar.

And if you're a connoisseur, I hope this book will lighten up your library with the sort of salacious anecdotes and goofy quotes that other books deem unfit for print.

=====

One quick note before you read any further: I'm not a professional historian, nor do I pretend to be. Whenever possible, I've double- and triple-sourced my facts to make sure you're getting reasonably accurate history and good advice. But if an expert on grappa or the British Navy reads this and becomes outraged at some minor inaccuracies, all I can say is, don't blame me. Blame my high school history teacher for instilling me with poor research skills.

Finally, I'll leave you with words from the most quoted person in history:

> *"Eat, drink, and be merry for tomorrow ye die—*
> *or wish ye were dead."* —ANONYMOUS

ALCOHOLICA
Esoterica

DOWN
THE HATCH

(THE WHAT, WHEN, WHERE, WHY, AND HOW OF ALCOHOL)

WHAT

"Alcohol—the cause of and solution to all of life's problems" —HOMER SIMPSON

"Fermentation may have been a greater discovery than fire." —DAVID RAINS WALLACE

Yeast poop. That's what you're drinking.

Yeast is a living creature; it's an airborne microscopic fungus that exists everywhere. In order to grow and multiply, it feeds on sugar, which it then excretes as two waste products: carbon dioxide (which gives beer and champagne their fizz) and alcohol.

Any alcohol that you drink has been produced by yeast feeding on the sugars in the base product (grape juice for wine, barley for beer, sugarcane for rum, etc.). Before Louis Pasteur figured out the science behind this process in the nineteenth century, the seemingly magical ability of a handful of yeast to convert a tub of grapes into wine led monks to only one conclusion—their name for yeast was "God-is-Good."

There are over three thousand varieties of yeast, each with its own unique properties. Because of this, brewers and distillers jealously guard the particular yeast they use to produce their drink. Some have carefully nurtured the same strain for centuries. In fact, when bourbon distilleries were shut during American Prohibition, many stored their trademark yeast cultures in local bakeries for the entire thirteen-year period rather than let them die.

WHEN

"It's always happy hour somewhere in the world, the rest is just good timing." —ANONYMOUS

"I shall drink no wine before its time! Okay, it's time." —GROUCHO MARX

Cocktail Hour

Between World Wars I and II, social customs started to loosen in America and England. Attire became a little more casual. And while people weren't exactly in T-shirts and jeans yet, they didn't have to spend two hours before dinner tightening their whalebone corsets and powdering their wigs. This left a big hole in people's schedule. Suddenly, the hours normally reserved for predinner primping (6:00 to 8:00 P.M.) were free. So why not have a drink?

The concept of a cocktail hour took hold. In the 1920s, America's grand hotels replaced their traditional English five o'clock teatime with cocktails. But because of Prohibition (and for etiquette's sake), the cocktail hour was referred to as "tea" up until the mid thirties, and some of the first American cocktail shakers were shaped like teapots.

Happy Hour

There's no record of who first started the practice of "happy hour" in bars, but the first time it appeared in print was in a newspaper article on July 4 (appropriately enough), 1961: "All went home happy except the Newport police . . . and those deprived of their happy hour at the cocktail bar" (*Providence Journal*, Rhode Island). The casual reference implies that the term was already known by that time.

Actually, the phrase "happy hours" was already in the English language by the late 1800s. People working in the world of London theater used "happy hours" as rhyming slang for "flowers." Whether there was any crossover between the hard-drinking theater crowd and the bar phrase is unknown.

Holidaze

Due to a combination of office parties, singles depression, and interaction with extended family, people drink more during the Christmas holidays than any other time of year. In December of 2003, New Yorkers consumed more than 3 million gallons of spirits. In comparison, they only managed 1.2 million gallons that February (for more on the December/Jesus/drink connection see "Lords of the Drink," page 189).

"Lunch"

In Middle Ages England, a noon meal tended to consist of a slice of bread and a lot of beer. The meal became known as a "nunchion," which combined the words "noon" and "scheken," which meant "noon drinking." This eventually turned to "luncheon" and "lunch."

WHERE

"You sit back in the darkness, nursing your beer, breathing in that ineffable aroma of the old-time saloon: dark wood, spilled beer, good cigars, and ancient whiskey—the sacred incense of the drinking man." —BRUCE AIDELLS

"No, sir: There is nothing which has yet been contrived by man by which so much happiness is produced as by a good tavern or inn." —SAMUEL JOHNSON

"A good local pub has much in common with a church, except that a pub is warmer, and there's more conversation." —WILLIAM BLAKE

Greece—the cradle of civilization and the birthplace of bars. At the same time, as a matter of fact. The Greeks developed two sorts of drinking spots: the symposium, where elite men like Plato, Socrates, and Aristotle gathered to drink and philosophize, and lower-class establishments where the common folk could gossip about discus throwing and nude olive-oil wrestling and such.

When the Romans came along, they weren't too hot on the intellectual symposiums, but they were all for the lower-class dives. They called them *tavernae*, and wherever Roman troops went (which was pretty much everywhere), *tavernae* began to appear, indicated by a garland of grapevine leaves hanging over the door.

More than anywhere else in the Roman empire, this concept took off in England, where people had been using clearings in the forests as drinking sites. Between the bad weather and their inordinate love of drink, the English decided that the invading Roman army was onto something. They began creating their own taverns. Grape leaves were a bit scarce in England, so people hung the long rods they used to mix beer, ale staffs, over their doors. Pretty soon, ale staffs were hanging everywhere and taverns had to distinguish themselves further with names and signs.

Taverns became a regular part of every town and a resting point for people passing through. And in the Middle Ages, a steady flow of traffic was beginning to move around the normally staid, agrarian English countryside—the concept of the pilgrimage had been born. It began when Thomas à Becket, the archbishop of Canterbury, was murdered inside his church. Religious rubberneckers began traveling from all over England to see the crime scene. The concept of visiting a holy site spread to include the death and birth sites of other saints around Europe.

These pilgrims were the first real tourists. They even spawned the invention of the souvenir—pin-on badges that pilgrims could buy showing they'd traveled to a particular holy site. And, of course, when the pilgrims got to these sites after weeks of walking, they wanted a beer and a bed. Monasteries realized they could make some easy dough and gave them both, creating overnight inns complete with breweries.

The taverns and these new inns were a hit. By the

early seventeenth century, England had over thirteen thousand alehouses, for a population of just 5 million. By way of comparison, England now has sixty thousand pubs for 60 million people. In the fledgling American colonies, they proved especially vital. A law was even passed requiring every American town to have a tavern in it (see "Early America: One Nation Under the Influence," page 216).

As the colonies expanded into a full-fledged (and thirsty) country, the American tavern became a catchall social center—an employment office, business boardroom, union hall, and political party headquarters. Its importance to the community meant that it could adapt to any conditions. In the Wild West, tents selling whiskey morphed into saloons. When Prohibition came along, they closed their front doors, opened the back doors, and became speakeasies. When yuppies came along, some ferns and carpets turned them into wine bars. The bar has become a creature Darwin would be proud of, forever evolving to meet the demands of its time and place, because people's demands are the same now as they were with the ancient Greeks. We all just want a place to sit and spend a leisurely afternoon, drinking and talking about the newest in nude olive-oil wrestling.

A Place by Any Other Name

A tavern also became known as an alehouse or a tap house. In the mid-seventeenth century, the phrase "public house" came into use, which in 1865 finally got shortened to "pub." Or as writer Charles Booth called it, "the primordial cell of British life."

Some other good names given to taverns have been: boozery, gin swamp, grog pond, dive, gin palace (see page 121), grog shop, toddy shop, honky-tonk, roadhouse, juke joint, speakeasy, and wine vault.

It's not too much of a brain twister to learn that

"bar" is short for "barrier," as in the thing that keeps the customers from getting at all the booze. It was shortened to bar at the end of the sixteenth century.

Bar Games

Alcohol and sports—the perfect combination. Before *Monday Night Football*, bars used any competition they could to keep people entertained (and gambling). In Elizabethan England, a tavern would host nights of badger baiting, bear baiting, ape baiting (!), cock-fights, dogfights, boxing, and wrestling. In nineteenth-century America, rat baiting was all the craze, and fights pitting one dog against a hundred rats could draw admission fees as high as $1.50. As a little comparison, a boxing match between two grown men would only cost 50 cents.

"WE HAD GONE OUT THERE TO PASS THE BEAUTIFUL DAY OF HIGH SUMMER LIKE TRUE IRISHMEN—LOCKED IN THE DARK SNUG OF A PUBLIC HOUSE." —BRENDAN BEHAN

A Good Puzzle

"A good puzzle would be to cross Dublin without passing a pub," wrote James Joyce in his novel *Ulysses*.

A radio station in Dublin recently took Joyce up on the challenge, offering a prize of $200 to any of their readers who could map a route through the city without passing a pub. The contest was thought to be unsolvable until someone proposed the following—travel any route you want, just don't pass up any pubs, go into every single one of them. This proved to be a fair and all-around enjoyable solution, and the prize money was awarded.

Sign of the Times

At the end of the fourteenth century, London began growing rapidly with a tangle of streets and alleyways popping up everywhere to accommodate the increase in traffic. King Richard II decided he had to impose some order on the chaotic expansion of the city, and the best way to do it would be to label every street with a name and a street sign. The problem was, most of the population were illiterate. So instead, Richard decided to go with what the population knew best. He ordered all taverns to hang signs with their name and logo outside their door. Order was restored to the city, allowing maps to be drawn and messages delivered, all thanks to taverns.

Word Origins

THERE'S NO SUCH THING AS A FREE LUNCH: This expression dates back to the nineteenth century, when American bars began giving away free (heavily salted) snacks to attract customers, who would then want to buy drinks.

SCOT-FREE: Beginning in the fourteenth century, the "scot" was a tax imposed on English taverns operating within the city limits. People who traveled to rural taverns for a cheaper drink were described as drinking "scot free."

WHY

*"The thirstiness of mankind is something supernatural.
We are forever drinking on one excuse or another. . . .
We drink the Queen, and the Army, and the ladies,
and everybody else that is drinkable; and, I believe, if
the supply ran short, we should drink our mothers-in-
law. . . . By the way, we never eat anybody's health,
always drink it. Why should we not stand up now and
then and eat a tart to somebody's success?"*
—J. K. JEROME

Mankind has never *needed* an excuse to drink, but then, having a good excuse doesn't hurt. Alcohol was originally a libation offered to and consumed in honor of the gods. So when drinking filtered down from religious ceremonies into everyday life, we simply switched from honoring the gods to honoring each other.

As for the concept of the toast itself, it stems from the fact that in ancient times, wine was pretty crappy. To improve its flavor, the Romans began dipping pieces of charred bread into their wine to absorb some of the sediment. As wine slowly improved, this practice faded, except in England, where the wine had to be imported. By the time the casks crossed the ocean, the wine had often deteriorated to the point where the burned bread remained necessary.

So the use of actual toast was common, but the concept of "toasting" only started in the late seventeenth century, during a festival in the posh health resort town of Bath, England. A young lady who was famed for her beauty was using the public baths and a crowd of admirers had gathered to watch. One young suitor was so bold as to take a glass of the water she was bathing in and drank to her health in front of the crowd. This prompted a drunk in the crowd to shout that he didn't care much for the gentleman's choice of liquor, but he would take the toast (i.e., the lady, who made the water drinkable by her presence). The crowd burst out laughing; the suitor was humiliated, and a popular term was coined.

The Origins of Tipping

The reason we started the practice of tipping people (a waiter, a bellboy, a surly coffeeshop employee) can be seen in the French word for it, *pourboire*, meaning "in order to drink." Originally, we were providing someone money so they could toast our health.

HOW

The Fine Art and Etiquette of Toasting

When imbibing, the Romans had to follow strict social guidelines known as *leges compotandi*, or "drinking laws." One of these laws stated that when toasting your sweetheart, you had to drink a cup of wine for every letter in her name.

Being great feasters and drinkers, the Vikings had even more complicated rituals regarding who, how, and when to toast, but the most important one (and one that has filtered down into the modern day) is that you had to look the person you were toasting in the eye. If not, you were considered a tricksy sort and might end up with an ax in your skull.

Skull damage is also responsible for the most time-honored tradition of the British Royal Navy—the toast to the health of the Crown. Unlike all other toasts, it's done sitting down. This stems from when the none-too-bright George III was a prince attending a ship's dinner belowdecks. He stood to lead the toast and cracked his head on a low-lying wooden beam. He swore that when he was king, the royal toast would be done while seated.

And in the American Wild West, it was not only polite but imperative to your physical well-being to drink your whiskey with your gun hand, thus showing your friendly intentions.

Clink

There are a number of theories explaining why we clink glasses with our companions before taking the first sip but there are a number of theories. And since no one knows the true origins of this tradition, there's no proof one way or another, they're all equally valid (or invalid, if you're a cynic).

Theory 1: Until the sixteenth century, people didn't have their own drinking vessel, they drank out of one large goblet that was passed around the table. Eventually, people got sick of sharing their social diseases and opted for individual glasses, but they clinked these together to symbolize the sharing of their drinks from the same vessel.

Theory 2: It started with the Vikings, who would bang their goblets together so that some of their drink would slosh over into the other person's goblet. This acted as a safeguard against poisoning—anyone who slipped a mickey in his neighbor's drink would get the poison right back in his own.

Theory 3: The clinking of the glass sounded like a church bell ringing, which scared away any evil spirits lurking in the drink.

Smash

The tradition of smashing a glass after a toast is based on the idea that to drink from that glass again would dilute the power of the original toast.

On the Perils of Overtoasting

King Philip the Handsome of Spain drank himself to death in 1506. His wife, Joanna, took no lessons from this and, in her grief, began drinking heavily herself. She never left the marital bed and kept Philip's body in bed with her as company, drinking toasts to his health every morning and night. She quickly earned the moniker "Joanna the Mad."

The smell finally prompted servants to remove Philip's corpse after Joanna passed out one night. But upon reviving, she took no notice of her husband's absence and continued toasting his health.

History's Most Expensive Toast

Sir Thomas Gresham earned top brown-nosing points with the royal court when he toasted the health of Queen Elizabeth I with a glass of wine in which he'd crushed a pearl that was worth £15,000 ($30,000).

A SAMPLING OF SALUTATIONS

"Cheers"

This popular British expression (and American sitcom) derive from the more formal toast, "May you be of good cheer."

"MAY THE SKIN OF YOUR ARSE NEVER BECOME THE HEAD OF A BANJO!"
—TRADITIONAL TOAST BY THE BRITISH ROYAL AIR FORCE

"One for My Homies"

Originated in American hip-hop culture in the late-twentieth century, this phrase is used to commemorate dead friends. It is uttered while pouring the first sip of a beer or malted beverage onto a street curb or the site of the late friend's demise. The tradition of remembering a friend with a drink dates back to the Vikings, who brewed special "memory ales" to honor comrades who had fallen in battle.

> "HERE'S LOOKING UP YOUR KILT."
> —TRADITIONAL SCOTTISH TOAST

> "May you be in heaven half an hour before the devil knows you're dead."
>
> "May you live to be a hundred years, with one extra year to repent." —TRADITIONAL IRISH TOASTS

BEER

A BRIEF HISTORY OF JOE SIX-PACK

> *"Without question, the greatest invention in the history of mankind is beer. Oh, I grant you that the wheel was also a fine invention, but the wheel does not go nearly as well with pizza."* —DAVE BARRY

Next time you're sitting on your couch with a beer, take a moment to consider this—you're not just having a drink. You're having *the* drink. Literally. The word "beer" comes from the Latin *biber*, meaning "to drink." Beer has been so integral to the history of mankind that it became synonymous with the very act of drinking.

The Lady Who Fills the Mouth

> *"The mouth of a perfectly happy man is filled with beer."* —ANCIENT EGYPTIAN WISDOM

Civilization began when the ancient Sumerians settled down to cultivate the land. But were they growing grain for food or so they could make more beer? In other words, was *beer* responsible for the creation of civilization? Some historians say yes, some say no, but, either way, it's a pretty good indication of beer's importance to early mankind.

Actually, I keep using the word "mankind," but in reality we owe beer to women. Because a woman's place was in the kitchen. And the very first beer in the history of the world was . . . <drum-roll> . . . a lump of bread dough left out too long.

Airborne yeast would have quickly gathered and begun fermentation. So by the time someone bit into that hunk of dough, it was packing enough of a buzz to make the Sumerians give it a closer look. Wine was around at the same time, or perhaps earlier, but wine was just a drink. This new thing, on the other hand, was something entirely different—beer came from bread. Beer was food. And not just to the ancient Sumerians.

> "WINE IS BUT SINGLE BROTH, ALE IS MEAT, DRINK, AND CLOTH."
> —Sixteenth-century English proverb

Beer's historical popularity stems largely from the fact that even up until the nineteenth century, it was a major source of nutrition (iron and B vitamins, especially). The Egyptian hieroglyphic symbol for food was a loaf of bread and a jug of beer. Plus, it was cheaper and more readily available than wine for the simple reason that fruit rots quickly while grain stores well. Beer became, by its very nature, a drink for the common folk.

The common folk were so thankful, they even invented a new god to be thankful to—Ninkasi, "the lady who fills the mouth" (the connection between women and beer is so strong that practically every culture with a beer-creation myth has a female god of beer, see "Lords of the Drink," page 189).

Sumerian women advanced from fermenting dough to fermenting the grain itself, which upped the alcohol content and allowed them more room for creativity. By 3000 B.C., people could choose between black beer, white beer, red beer, mother beer, beer from the netherworld, beer for the sacrifice, beer for the supper, beer with horns, and beer with a head.

With beer well and truly invented, it was time to create its handmaiden, beer-drinking culture, and for that we turn to the Egyptians.

> "IN MY OPINION, MOST OF THE GREAT MEN OF THE PAST WERE ONLY THERE FOR THE BEER."
> —A.J.P. TAYLOR, BRITISH HISTORIAN

My Liver Wears a Dress

Up and down the Fertile Crescent, people were chugging like frat boys, and none more so than the Egyptians. They dedicated a full 40 percent of their grain crop to beer, because for them it wasn't just food and drink. It was used as medicine. It was used as currency to pay the stonemasons who built the pyramids. They even managed to invent a few customs that we still associate with beer today.

- **Advertising:**

    "Drink Eblan—the beer with the heart of a lion."
    —STONE TABLET, 3000 B.C.

- **Breasts:** Brewers would lure men into their shops by decorating the exterior with carvings of curvaceous bare-breasted maidens holding curvaceous jugs of beer, curvaceously.

- **Drinking Songs:**

"When I have abundance of beer,
I feel great. I feel wonderful.
By the beer, I am happy
My heart is full of joy, my liver is full of luck.
When I am full of gladness, my liver wears the dress
befitting a queen."

—An actual inscription dating from
2000 b.c. Seriously.

Beer informed every part of their culture. So it's no surprise that when mankind's first written laws were laid down in 1700 b.c. in the Code of Hammurabi, beer warranted a few regulations:

Barmaids who served mugs that weren't filled to the top were put to death by drowning. Brewers who overcharged customers were put to death by drowning. And brewers who committed the most egregious act of all, producing beer of low quality, were put to death by drowning, but with a twist—they were drowned in their own inferior beer.

Not everyone took beer this seriously, as the Egyptians discovered when they began exporting it. The other side of the Mediterranean was wine country and the Greeks were less than impressed. After sampling some, the physician Dioskorides complained (for the first but certainly not the last time in history) that beer caused too frequent urination.

Ditto with the Romans. Emperor Julian even trash-talked beer with a poem:

"Who made you and from what?
By the true Bacchus [wine] I know you not.
He smells of nectar.
You smell of goat."

But when the Roman empire began advancing across Europe, they discovered that beer *had* found some customers north of the Alps, where grapes didn't grow, in the land of the barbarians.

BEER   17

Alewives Meet the Brothers

Actually, "barbarian" meant "anyone not Roman," including the Vikings, the Teutons, and especially the Celts. And they took to beer like, well, like barbarians. In A.D. 21, the Roman scribe Strabo wrote with some admiration that "their casks are larger than houses."

They also took the traditions of the Egyptians. Beer was woman's work, and alewives were much respected. Women were allowed legal ownership of their brewing equipment. The king of Hordoland even chose his queen because of her skills as a brewer.

But not everyone had the king's options. Most men were stuck in marriages with women who couldn't brew their way out of a paper bag. So they found women in their village who *could* make a decent beer and paid them for their services.

"GIVE ME A WOMAN WHO LOVES BEER AND I WILL CONQUER THE WORLD."
–KAISER WILHELM

The alewife made good money from her trade and enjoyed respect in the community, but that respect came at a price—even one batch of bad ale could earn them, by law, a severe fine or a dunking in the village pond. And that was just in *this* life. A stone carving in a church in Ludlow, England, shows the fate of an alewife who dared to cheat her customers—demons cast her into hell.

But by the eleventh century, even honest alewives weren't long for this world, because the next great empire to conquer Europe was the boys-only club known as the Catholic Church.

Monks drank beer for the same reason as normal folk—food. While monastery abbots were making money by the handful and kicking it up to the Church, the monks, with their vows of poverty, barely had enough to eat. So to ensure proper nutrition, they rationed themselves a hearty five *liters* of beer a day.

With the resources of the Catholic Church at their disposal, the monks could brew enough for themselves and more. A lot more. They began selling their excess beer and suddenly the Church saw dollar signs. Huge monastic breweries were constructed next to rivers with water wheels to power the production. In contrast, alewives worked out of their kitchens with nothing more than a pot and a stirring stick. They didn't stand a chance.

By 1086, the monks at Saint Paul's Cathedral in London were brewing almost 68,000 gallons of ale a year. Medieval Germany alone had four to five hundred monastic breweries. And while monks made many of the great strides forward in brewing, most people never knew about it.

Monasteries made several beers. The premium stuff warranted names like Merry-Go-Down and Dragon's Milk, and it was reserved exclusively for abbots and distinguished guests. The general public and the lowly monks who actually did the brewing only merited the weakest 3 percent beer. Shakespeare called it "small beer," but most people used a less charitable name, "starve-gut."

"THE SELLING OF BAD BEER IS A CRIME AGAINST CHRISTIAN LOVE." —EDICT FROM THE CITY OF AUGSBURG, THIRTEENTH CENTURY

People didn't have a choice, though. The Church owned the breweries, the barley fields, the spice fields, and even the inns where beer was sold. It had an almost total monopoly on European beer for the next three hundred years, a stranglehold that was only broken by the arrival of an evil weed and the death of 25 million people.

> *"Beer is not a good cocktail party drink, especially in a home where you don't know where the bathroom is."*—BILLY CARTER, BROTHER OF PRESIDENT JIMMY CARTER AND MAKER OF "BILLY BEER"

Wicked and Pernicious Weed

Before we go any further, I should stop for a moment and apologize. Up to this point, I've been using the words "beer" and "ale" interchangeably, but in medieval times, they were very, very different things. Beer was made with hops. Ale was made without hops.

So what the hell *is* hops exactly?

Well, it's a leafy vine plant that is (brace yourselves, stoners) a member of the cannabis family. Without its citric bitter flavor, modern beer drinkers probably wouldn't even recognize the taste of medieval ale. Ale was heavily spiced with honey, pepper, rosemary, cinnamon, powdered crab claws, anything that came along, really. So when some Bohemian brewers came across the hops plant in the ninth century, they experimented with it the way they did with any other flavoring. And they discovered something fantastic—hops was a natural preservative.

Ale spoiled after two weeks. Beer could last a month. And because of hops's strong flavor, brewers could use less malt, which meant they could make twice as much beer at a tenth of the cost of ale. It was a godsend to brewers.

But not to the Church. The spices that flavored ale were big business and the Church owned that business. Hops made the need for spices obsolete, so they kept a tight lid on its use. And considering the Church monopolized the ale industry, that lid was pretty tight. Hops was kept hostage in Germany for centuries, until people became too preoccupied with coughing up blood to care what went into beer.

In the fourteenth century, a sickly flea bit a human. A few decades later, one-third of Europe was dead. The bubonic plague killed men and monks alike, and monasteries became so short of manpower that they couldn't meet the demand for ale. Commercial brewers stepped in, and the secret of hops got out.

The elite tried to stop its spread—the archbishop of Cologne attempted to outlaw hops; Russian archduke Vasil II and Henry VIII both banned it; burghers in Shrewsbury, England, were reduced to out-and-out name-calling, labeling it "a wicked and pernicious weed."

But all for naught. By the sixteenth century, the higher quality and cheaper prices created by hops had permanently altered the public's taste. The old ale was dead; modern beer was born.

Entire Butt

Beer was a brave new world, and the British led the way, partly due to their rich tradition of brewing, partly due to their position as a world power, and mostly because they were great big drunks. Seriously.

In 1684, 28 percent of the nation's economy was

dedicated to beer (to say nothing of hard liquor). The seventeenth, eighteenth, and nineteenth centuries were not temperate times. The twentieth century is up for debate as well.

British tastes hadn't totally moved on from ale. The popular beer was "three-threads," a combination of the old sweet ale, the new bitter beer, and a weaker beer to water it down. But three-threads was a pain in the ass. To pour even one pint required three different kegs of beer. The challenge was to copy its taste with a single beer.

> "NOTHING EVER TASTED ANY BETTER THAN A COLD BEER ON A BEAUTIFUL AFTERNOON WITH NOTHING TO LOOK FORWARD TO BUT MORE OF THE SAME." —HUGH HOOD

The answer came in 1722—Entire Butt (so named because it only needed one barrel, or "butt"). And with a vigorous 7 percent alcohol, it was an instant success, becoming such a staple of working-class life that it was nicknamed for the most common job in London at the time, the porter.

But porter beer wasn't just popular in a conventional sense. It was a popularity of historic proportions. It was the dawn of the Industrial Age, and the English countryside was migrating into the cities in search of work. London became the most populous city in the world. The drunkest, too (see "Gin," page 114).

Beer brewers became beer barons, and they flaunted their newfound wealth in the age-old tradition—by trying to swing a bigger dick than the next guy. For instance, in 1814, the Meux Horseshoe Brewery in London built a brewing vat that was 160 feet wide and 23 feet high, with an interior big enough to seat two hundred for dinner, which is how its completion was celebrated. Why two hundred? Because a rival brewer, Henry Thale, had built a vat that seated one hundred.

After the festivities, the vat was filled to its twenty-thousand barrel (1 million pints) capacity. Given the grand scale of the project, it's easy to see how they could have overlooked the hairline fracture in its side. The only worker who did notice didn't pay it much mind. The explosion was heard five miles away.

A wall of beer washed down the street, caving in two buildings and killing eight people by "drowning, injury, poisoning by the porter fumes or drunkenness." Rescue attempts were blocked by the thousands who flocked to the area to drink directly off the road. And when survivors were finally pulled from the beer and brought to the hospital, the other patients became convinced from the smell that the hospital was serving beer to every other ward but them. A riot broke out.

This was a city that really liked its porter.

But as British brewers carried on competing for the public's attention by making their beer stronger, darker, stouter, a revolution was brewing down in Bavaria and Bohemia. And, yes, I know that's a terrible pun.

Testicle Yeast

Summer in Central Europe was a dull time to be a brewer. Yeast wouldn't function in the heat, so brewers had to close down until fall. But in the fifteenth century, some Bavarian monks with a serious jones for beer decided to move their entire operation underground into the cool, ice-filled caves of the Alps.

Right away, strange things started happening. Remember, yeast is a living creature, so it reacted to the cold the same way a man's testicles do in an icy shower. Instead of frothing up at the top of the beer as usual, it shrank back, down to the bottom of the barrel. And instead of taking a few days, it took weeks to ferment. So the monks stored the beer in the caves (which earned it the name *lager*, from the German word "to store") until it was finished. The result was a cleaner, better-tasting beer.

This was great news for beer lovers, but it wasn't real handy for anyone who didn't live near ice-filled caves. Plus, people were just flat-out resistant to change. Cologne (which was proving itself quite the xenophobic little burg after banning hops) considered lager too intoxicating; it banned cold fermentation. 90 percent of all German breweries stuck to warm fermentation because . . . well . . . just because.

> "Quaintest thoughts, queerest fancies come to life and fade away.
> What care I how time advances; I am drinking ale today."
> —EDGAR ALLAN POE

After four hundred years of this, some brewers from the town of Pilsen, Bohemia, became fed up with the old ways. By the nineteenth century, the breweries were increasingly antiquated and the town's beer quality was declining. The final straw came when an entire batch of the town's beer was declared unfit to drink. It was just too much for these beer-proud people. An angry mob dumped the offending barrels onto the steps of the city hall and declared their intention to start a new brewery, one that broke with tradition and utilized the latest science had to offer.

It was good timing. Science suddenly had a lot to offer. Louis Pasteur had discovered the secrets of yeast. Ice machines had been invented. A sympathetic monk smuggled them some top-secret high-quality yeast from Bavaria, and they hired a brewer with knowledge of cold fermentation. They did everything right, but things *still* went wrong.

An accident occurred in the brewery and instead of the lager coming out a fine dark hue as it always had before, it came out a light, golden color. The date was October 5, 1842. They called it pilsner.

It's not just that pilsner was lighter and more refreshing than porter, it *looked* better, too. In the mid-1800s, Europeans began drinking out of clear glasses rather than the traditional wooden or metal mugs. And a glass of porter looked like mud, but pilsner winked and sparkled in the light.

The revolution was immediate. 90 percent of beer in the world today is a pilsner. Unfortunately, most of that 90 percent is barely even beer.

One Beer to Rule Them All

"Why is American beer served cold? So you can tell it from urine." —DAVID MOULTON

All over the world, public taste migrated from dark English porter to light German and Czech pilsner. But at the same time, many German and Czech brewers were migrating from beer-devout Europe to the heathen new land of America.

They set up shop in Milwaukee, where the endless supply of ice from the Great Lakes enabled them to set up their cold-fermentation breweries. In 1850, there were 431 breweries in operation. By 1873, America was the proud owner of a record 4,131 breweries.

But the good times ended in 1880, when Anheuser-Busch launched the first fleet of refrigerated railroad cars, enabling its beer to travel to every corner of the country. Budweiser became America's first national-brand "beer." Smaller breweries began closing, bought out or run out of business.

And then, in 1920, the hammer came down—Prohibition. Only the very biggest breweries were able to survive the thirteen-year dry spell. Most scraped along producing nonalcoholic beers with names that made them sound like a Mexican boy-band: Lux-o, Famo, Vivo, Bevo, and Pablo. Anheuser-Busch converted its breweries into ice cream factories and produced 1 million gallons a year. The smaller breweries were swept off the board altogether.

So no one was left to challenge the major breweries when they instituted a nationwide shift in beer during World War II. With America's men off fighting, beer was marketed toward women by making it lighter and lighter in taste (which also make it cheaper and cheaper to produce). Only, when the war ended, the reign of light beer didn't.

Now, cut-rate beer *does* have its own charms. Namely, cost. But with that said, it's a sad day when cheap, crappy beer is the *only* option. And, in 1978, that's the situation America found itself in with a grand total of eighty-nine breweries producing just twenty-five national brands of beer.

"YOU CAN'T HAVE A REAL COUNTRY UNLESS YOU HAVE A BEER AND AN AIRLINE—IT HELPS IF YOU HAVE SOME KIND OF A FOOTBALL TEAM, OR SOME NUCLEAR WEAPONS, BUT AT THE VERY LEAST YOU NEED A BEER."—FRANK ZAPPA

But in 1965, Fritz Maytag, the twenty-seven-year-old heir to the Maytag washing machine fortune, decided to use his inheritance for good instead of evil. He bought the failing Anchor Brewery in San Francisco, and dedicated it to the unusual concept of high-quality beer.

He unwittingly sparked the microbrewery movement (a trend that was echoed by England's Campaign for Real Ale) and there are now nearly two thousand breweries in operation in the United States, more than anywhere else in the world. Mind you, microbrews aren't exactly a major revolution. All combined, they're a whopping 2 percent of the market (Budweiser alone is 50 percent, add Miller and Coors and it's in the nineties). But what they *do* provide is something there hadn't been in a long time—choice.

And for beer, the drink that made its mark on history by being the most democratic of all drinks, the drink of the common man, having the ability to choose is the most basic right of all.

USELESS INFO

Good Governing

In 1809, American president James Madison attempted to establish a national brewery. He also wanted to appoint a new position to his cabinet—the secretary of beer. Sadly, he failed on both counts.

Blessed Beer Babies

Beer was so popular with medieval priests and monks that in the thirteenth century, they stopped baptizing children with holy water and started using beer.

The Ample Alewife

What did alewives look like? Well, one indication comes from a type of herring that's also known as "alewife." Apparently, early New England fishermen gave it this name because of the herring's remarkably large belly.

Fun with Numbers

- 7 percent of Ireland's barley crop goes to the production of Guinness beer. 10 percent of America's entire rice crop is devoted to beer.

- 63 percent of those who drink inexpensive beer are men.

- 43 percent of the cost of every bottle of beer sold in the United States goes toward federal, state, and local taxes.

- 77 percent of British men know how much their favorite beer costs, but only 38 percent know the correct size of their girlfriend and/or wife's bra.

Brew Witch

If alewives were responsible for brewing, it stood to reason that when a batch went wrong, it was also the fault of a woman—a brew witch. Vats of beer were often adorned with charms and amulets to ward off evil, but if they persisted in spoiling, the villagers had themselves a good old-fashioned witch burning. The last recorded burning of a brew witch took place in 1591.

The Longest Word in Beer

Koeniglichbayerischeroberbiersteuerhaupteinkassierer. This was the official title of the royal Bavarian beer-tax collector.

Fishy Beer

Isinglass is a substance used by many modern brewers to clarify beer at the end of fermentation. It's a gelatin made from the bladders of sturgeon. How someone first came to associate sturgeon bladders with clean beer is an interesting question to ponder.

1,001 Pints

The nineteenth-century British were ingenious at inventing occasions that merited a beer. There were child ales, change-of-place ales, journey ales, walking stick ales, cuckoo ales, holy ales (see page 197), foot ales, groaning ales (see pages 201), dirge ales, soul ales, and, starting all the way back in the eleventh century, bride ales, to celebrate a marriage. "Bride ale" was shortened to "bridal," and became another name for the entire wedding feast before it took its modern form in "bridal shower," "bridal gown," "bridal gift," etc.

Growler, Bottle, Can

In the days before beer was sold in bottles (1850s) and cans (1935), people who wanted a beer at home had to go down to the local pub with a galvanized pail and fill-'er-up. This became known as a "growler," reputedly because the beer sloshing around in the pail caused a strange growling sound as the CO_2 escaped through the lid.

Strange Brew

One of the most popular ale flavorings in medieval England was wormwood, the psychoactive plant used in neon-green absinthe (see "Absinthe," page 181). So it's likely that medieval beer drinking was a much more colorful experience than it is today.

Clear as a Mountain Spring

Long have brewers emphasized the importance of water to a truly good beer. Only in previous centuries, their priorities were a little bit different.

The 1702 *Brewer's Guide to London* offered this advice

on how to brew a good strong ale: "Thames water taken up about Greenwich at low-water when it is free from all the brackishness of the sea and it has all the fat and sullage [sewage] of this great city of London, makes very strong drink.

"It will all itself ferment wonderfully and after its due purgations and three times stinking, it will be so strong that several Sea Commanders have told me that it has often fuddled their mariners."

USEFUL INFO

"It's very hard to get pretentious about beer. You can become knowledgeable and start to talk with a high-falutin' vocabulary. But you can only go so far with beer, and I've always liked that." —FRITZ MAYTAG, ANCHOR BREWERY

Check Your Head

For an ale, the ideal head is one finger's worth. Otherwise, the much-desired bitter hop oils are drawn out of the beer by the foam. Conversely, for a pilsner, the head *should* foam up over the head of the glass to kill some of the bitterness in the beer and to allow the aroma to really bloom (although spillage will occur before pouring, mastery is achieved).

And anyone who's spent five minutes waiting for a Guinness will tell you that stout needs to be poured in two parts to allow time for the head (a finger and a half's worth) to get as thick and creamy as possible.

Tasting

"A fine beer may be judged with only one sip, but it is better to be sure." —CZECH PROVERB

Good news, beer drinkers! When you're tasting beer, there's none of this effete sipping that wine drinkers use. Experts evaluate beer with the same preliminary look, swirl, sniff routine, but when it comes to the actual drinking, the taste buds that register beer's bitterness are located at the back of the tongue, so only a good hearty swallow will reach them.

Malt versus Hops

Beer tasters throw around descriptions like malty and hoppy quite a bit. Only, I don't know what either actually tastes like. I've never been in a store where I could sample a malt or a hop by itself. So the best way to know what the hell they're talking about is to try two beers from the extreme ends of the spectrum: double bocks are extremely malty, and bitter ales are very hoppy.

THE FAMILY TREE

There are as many permutations to beer as there are breweries, which is to say tens of thousands. But some of the basic categories are:

LAGER: Includes pilsner and bock beer. The bottom fermentation gives them a cleaner, crisper, more floral flavor and high carbonation. Pilsner and the majority of lagers are golden-colored and medium-bodied with a low alcohol content (around 3 percent). Bocks and double bocks, on the other hand, are potent (5 to 7 percent), sweet, highly malted affairs that tend to appeal to Germans and beer lovers only.

ALE: Includes amber ale, pale ale (and its subvariety, IPA), and bitter. This traditional English beer has the widest range of colors and tastes, but overall they tend

to have little carbonation and a fruity flavor that min-
gles with a bitter, highly hopped aftertaste. The combination of flavors makes it a complex beer, and most
microbreweries are judged by the quality of their first
ale.

PORTER: Includes stout. Porter is actually a type of
ale in which the malt has been roasted first, resulting
in the dark, almost black color. Stout, usually associated with Guinness, is the strongest, most full-bodied
version of porter. Both have chocolaty, coffee flavors.

WHEAT BEER: More common to Europe, as it
tends to be served with a piece of fruit, thus arousing
suspicions of girliness in Americans. Wheat beer is
thought to be the most refreshing summertime beer
due to its tart citrus and clove flavors. They can be
highly carbonated and strong, as yeast in the bottle
causes them to undergo a second fermentation, which
is what causes their cloudiness.

Skunked

You open your beer and a funky, skunky sort of smell
comes out. It doesn't happen *too* often, but you'll
come across it at least a few times in your life and it'll
probably be with a beer in a clear glass bottle. The reason for this is sunlight. Ultraviolet rays convert the
hop oils in beer into a rancid-smelling chemical.
That's why most premium beers come in dark bottles,
to keep the sun out.

It also explains the one basic rule of storing beer:
keep it in a cool, dark place.

W.C. Fields

(1880–1946)

W.C. Fields has become one of the most enduring icons in film, and he did it by inventing a character as archetypal as the white knight and the damsel in distress—the drunk. He's the bulbous-nosed curmudgeon whose attempts at enjoying a drink are under constant assault from such dreaded creatures as children, dogs, wives, and whatever else the cruel world throws his way. But with a heart.

Born William Claude Dukenfield, the son of Cockney-English immigrants, he ran away from home at the age of eleven to live on the streets of Philadelphia. To earn money, he picked up juggling and distinguished his act by adding comedic banter. By the age of fourteen, he was appearing on vaudeville stages in America and Europe as "The Tramp Juggler."

By 1915, he was one of the stars of the famous revue *Ziegfeld Follies,* on Broadway. His comedy routines proved so successful that his juggling became secondary, and in 1924, he had his own Broadway show. He appeared in several silent films, but it was the advent of sound that made him famous.

The silent film stars couldn't handle dialogue. Hollywood needed new stars. Comics like Fields and the Marx Brothers had spent years honing their acts on the vaudeville stage, so when the silent stars faded, the vaudevillians were able to jump into the pictures with road-tested dialogue ready to go. For Fields, this late arrival to stardom actually worked to his advantage, as his age now fit perfectly with his persona as a world-weary drunk.

The persona wasn't far from the real thing. He was reputed to keep $20,000 worth of booze stashed in his attic at all times, "in case Prohibition comes back," he quipped. Unlike many comedians, Fields wrote his own screenplays and improvised many of his best lines during the course of shooting. His best movies (which still hold up fairly well) include *You Can't Cheat an Honest Man, My Little Chick-adee, The Bank Dick,* and *Never Give a Sucker an Even Break.*

On Drinking

"I exercise extreme self-control. I never drink anything stronger than gin before breakfast."

"I cook with wine, sometimes I even add it to the food."

"A woman drove me to drink, and I'll be a son of a gun but I never even wrote to thank her."

"Christmas at my house is always at least six or seven times more pleasant than anywhere else. We start drinking early. And while everyone else is seeing only one Santa Claus, we'll be seeing six or seven."

"I drink with impunity . . . or anyone else who invites me."

On Not Drinking

"Now don't say you can't swear off drinking; it's easy. I've done it a thousand times."

"Back in my rummy days, I would tremble and shake for hours upon arising. It was the only exercise I got."

"I like to keep a bottle of stimulant handy in case I see a snake, which I also keep handy."

"During one of my treks through Afghanistan, we lost our corkscrew. We were compelled to live on food and water for several days."

On Hangovers

"I feel like a midget with muddy feet had been walking over my tongue all night."

On His Rationale for Not Drinking Water

"Fish fuck in it."

WINE

THE DRINK OF THE GODS
COMES DOWN TO EARTH

"We hear of the conversion of water into wine at the marriage in Cana as of a miracle. But this conversion is, through the goodness of God, made every day before our eyes. Behold the rain which descends from heaven upon our vineyards, and which incorporates itself with the grapes, to be changed into wine; a constant proof that God loves us, and loves to see us happy." —BEN FRANKLIN

That Old-Time Religion

For forty days and forty nights, the Lord covered the earth with water. And when the ark finally came to rest on dry land, the first thing Noah did to thank the Lord was get down on his knees, plant grapes, make wine, and then get good and loaded.

Whenever wine and ancient man came together, religious devotion seemed to spring forth. Wine and beer have been around since the first civilization (5400 B.C. is the earliest evidence), but while they both inspired devotion, they led very separate lives.

Beer was a cheaply made drink for the common man, but wine . . . the name is thought to come from the Sanskrit word *vena*, meaning "love." And like any kind of love you have to buy, it didn't come cheap. Grapes had to be carefully tended, pruned, and picked, and they spoiled rapidly. It was a drink for the gods, because only the god-kings and the priests could afford it.

This held true for every civilization/religion that sprang up around the Middle East at the time. Wine became a sacred drink, a symbol of God's love and the rich life. Pharaohs were buried with jars of wine for their journey to the afterlife, which resembled frat parties—paintings inside Egyptian tombs show heavenly wine-drinking sessions complete with vomiting and people being carted away, unconscious.

On a slightly more mature level, the Jewish religion incorporated it into their ceremonies and mythology. After the Jews had wandered the desert for forty years, an advance party returned one day with a bunch of grapes so large it took two men to carry it. They'd found the Promised Land.

The Greeks agreed. When wine reached their shores in 1600 B.C., they even formed a whole new religion around it, one that proved powerful enough to change the calendars and transform the world.

The Blood and the Body

"Religions change, but beer and wine remain."
—ANONYMOUS

On Greek soil, grapes grew with an abundance and ease that never existed back in the Middle East. Wine became available to rich and poor alike. So festivals invoking Dionysus, the god of wine, weren't just celebrated by an elite few priests, as they were in Middle Eastern religions; they were mass, drunken orgies.

The celebrations became so chaotic that in the fifth century, the leaders of Athens built an enclosed arena to host them and contain the damage. It was the first theater, and the festivals became the origin of all drama. The first play ever performed there was *The Bacchae*, in which Dionysus's female groupies become so crazed that they sacrifice their own sons. And the word "comedy" actually derives from *komos*, one of the ritual dances around a giant phallic symbol (which, if you think about it, isn't too different from most comedy today).

> "GIVE ME WINE TO WASH ME CLEAN OF THE WEATHER-STAINS OF CARE."
>
> —RALPH WALDO EMERSON

The timing of the festivals and the actual mythology of Dionysus were based around the stages of wine making. The harvest of the grapes in December symbolized Dionysus's body being torn apart (the grapes plucked from their bunch) and crushed into juice. Then at another festival in spring, his "body" would be resurrected in the form of the finished wine, and women would drink it on mountaintops while dancing and singing wildly in hopes of raising his spirit from the dead.

When the Greeks introduced wine to southern Italy, the Italians liked it so much they imported its god as well, with a few minor alterations. The moody Dionysus turned into the happier, cherubic Bacchus. They also took the mythology the next logical step by making Bacchus the actual god of resurrection, with the gift of bringing new life to any party. One legend of Bacchus told of a wedding feast at which he turned the water into wine.

And if all this sounds remarkably like the basic mythology of Christ, well, you're right. Early Christians readily admitted to fusing the life of Jesus with the mythology of Dionysus. The original Passion Play lifted whole passages from *The Bacchae* (in which, remember, a son was sacrificed). But all that would come in the A.D. years.

Before Christ, Bacchus was just one aspect of the wine culture Italians imported from Greece along with their vines and vinicultural skills. All of this was done as quickly as possible, because Italy had to feed the voracious appetite of the monster growing in the north—Rome.

> *"Wine is . . .*
> *. . . bottled poetry"*—ROBERT LOUIS STEVENSON
> *. . . sunlight, held together by water."*—GALILEO
> *. . . the discoverer of secrets."*—OLD AMERICAN PROVERB

Rising Falling Rome

"All right, but apart from the sanitation, the medicine, education, wine, public order, irrigation, roads, a fresh water system, and public health, what have the Romans ever done for us?" —REG, LEADER OF THE PEOPLE'S FRONT OF JUDEA, *MONTY PYTHON'S LIFE OF BRIAN*

It's hard to get our heads around the enormity of the Roman empire in modern times. It ruled Europe and beyond for over six hundred years, twice as long as the United States has even been an independent nation, much less a superpower. Rome itself had a population of over 1 million people. It took until the 1800s, almost two thousand years later, for a Mediterranean city (Naples) to reach that population again.

To feed a city of this size, the Romans invested heavily in the cultivation of both grain and grapes. Actually, they went a little overboard with the grapes. In A.D. 96, Emperor Domitian halted the planting of any new vineyards for fear there wouldn't be enough land to grow food on. This order was eventually re-scinded in A.D. 278 by Emperor Probus to keep his army happy.

The Roman army didn't march on its stomach so much as on its liver. Grapevines were considered vital supplies. That way, after conquering local armies, they could plant vineyards and be in vino as soon as possible.

"I CANNOT HELP WINCING AS I DRINK. ASCENT OF FLOWERS, RADIANCE AND HEAT, ARE DISTILLED HERE TO A FIERY, YELLOW LIQUID. JUST BEHIND MY SHOULDER-BLADES SOME DRY THING, WIDE-EYED, GENTLY CLOSES, GRADUALLY LULLS ITSELF TO SLEEP. THIS IS RAPTURE. THIS IS RELIEF."—VIRGINIA WOOLF

Wine wasn't a totally foreign concept to the rest of Europe. Traders had already shopped it around, but it was so expensive that only chieftains could afford it. The going price in Gaul was one human slave for one twenty-five-liter jug of wine, "thus exchanging the drink for the cup-bearer," noted one Roman scribe. But the arrival of Roman vineyards changed all that.

Wine became more commonly available and the conquered tribes even got into the spirit of things. The Romans had been using clay jugs to hold their wine, but the Celts took the wooden barrels they'd created to pour hot tar onto their enemies' heads and converted them into wine containers. A relative calm settled over the empire, and the art of wine making was able to flourish.

Uninterrupted by tribal skirmishes that disrupted growing seasons, Roman wine makers were able to an-alyze the growth of grapes over centuries. They became amazingly sophisticated—classifying grape varieties, seasonal, and soil preferences; and developing pruning, irrigation, and fertilization techniques to improve the flavor. And combining corks with the Celts' barrels, they were able to age wines and create vintages.

But the empire that lived by its wine also died by it. The alcohol slowly dissolved the lead from the Romans' drinking cups into their wine. Men went mad, and women became infertile; the ruling classes literally went extinct, and by A.D. 500, the empire imploded.

It's hard to imagine in our information age, but when the empire died, centuries of knowledge died with it. Wine making was an oral tradition, so when Romans withdrew from Europe, the vineyards fell silent.

Only a century later, wine was dealt another heavy blow when the prophet Muhammad spread Islam and its antialcohol ideology throughout the Middle East. Vineyards were torn up from the very soil that had given birth to wine thousands of years before.

Wine was dead in the Middle East; wine was dead in Europe. But Rome bequeathed one lasting legacy to its empire that would prove wine's salvation—Christianity.

> "[Wine can] light up candelabras in the brain, to illuminate all history and solve the secret of the destiny of man."
> —GEORGE MEREDITH

The Re-Resurrection

The word "wine" appears in the Bible 161 times, "vineyards" get mentioned 72 times, and "vines" 57. With a mixture of Dionysian myth and Judaic wine rituals, Christianity was one *seriously* wine-intensive religion.

But Christianity was just one of many different religions kicking around Rome at the time. That changed in A.D. 313, when the emperor Constantine converted.

And, in 380, Emperor Theodosius went a step further and declared it the official religion of Rome, making all other religions illegal. Churches and monasteries were established throughout Europe.

When Roman vineyards stopped operating, the monks had to make their own sacramental wine, but they had to start from scratch, relearning everything the Romans had lost. This wasn't helped by the chaos left in the wake of the passing empire.

Italy was under constant siege from warring tribes. Spain was under Islamic rule until the fifteenth century. And Germans liked wine but, what with being German and all, their monks preferred beer. France was wine's only hope.

> "GOD, IN HIS GOODNESS, SENT THE GRAPES
> TO CHEER BOTH GREAT AND SMALL;
> LITTLE FOOLS WILL DRINK TOO MUCH
> AND GREAT FOOLS NONE AT ALL."
>
> —ANONYMOUS

One monk in particular helped the cause—Saint Martin of Tours, the patron saint of wine (although his donkey took most of the credit, see "Saint Martin of Tours," page 194). Saint Martin proposed that *every* church and monastery become self-sufficient by establishing its own vineyard.

As the Church grew into a wealthy, land-owning empire, vineyards soon covered half of Europe, including some of the world's most famous wine regions like Burgundy and Bordeaux. And wine likes empires. With all that land to work with and the permanence of place afforded by the monasteries, French monks were able to reconstruct the Roman's knowledge—growing and analyzing centuries' worth of grapes and wine.

French wine was soon deemed so superior that several popes moved out of Rome altogether and set up shop in France. When someone suggested to Pope Urban V that he needed to return to the Vatican, the pope wailed, "There is no [Burgundy] wine in Italy, and without [Burgundy] wine how unhappy we would be."

Wine—the French stuff, at least—was nearly back to its full Roman glory, and it only took until the twelfth century, another six hundred years, to do it. In the interim, wine had effectively disappeared from Europe's cultural landscape. Beer had taken its place. But in the twelfth century, wine shot back into favor when Burgundy received an order for 1 million cases of wine a year.

The English had discovered wine.

The Poshing of Wine

Along with jumbo shrimp and army intelligence, English wine is one of the great oxymorons. The Romans *had* established vineyards there like everywhere else, but by the twelfth century, the English let them die altogether. Why bother? They could import from France. After all, they owned the place.

When King Henry II married Eleanor of Aquitane in 1152, her dowry was the entire southwest of France, including the vineyards of Bordeaux. So the royal court drank wine. France eventually reclaimed the region three hundred years later, but by then tradition had set in. The English aristocracy were wine drinkers. Not that the wine was any good. It was still being shipped in barrels, and would often spoil on the rough sea voyage to England.

"In vino veritas."
(In wine there is truth.)
—Plato

One visiting French courtier was horrified at what the English were drinking: "The wine is turned sour or mouldy—thick, greasy, stale, flat, and smacking of pitch. I have sometimes even seen great lords served with wine so muddy that a man must close his eyes and clench his teeth, wry-mouth and shuddering, and filtering the stuff rather than drinking."

It wasn't pleasant, but it was hip. And they drank this way until the late 1600s, when the solution to shipping wine finally arrived—cork, what the Romans had pioneered and then forgotten about over a thousand years before. The difference was revolutionary. With airtight bottles, wine wouldn't go bad, which allowed for the creation of vintages—storing a bottle for years to improve its flavor, rarity, and price. Wine became a collector's hobby.

> "THE SPIRIT OF WINE
> SANG IN MY GLASS, AND I LISTENED
> WITH LOVE TO HIS ODOROUS MUSIC,
> HIS FLUSHED AND MAGNIFICENT SONG."
> —WILLIAM ERNEST HENLY

All of this coincided with the height of Britain's empire, and England's elite had vast wealth to indulge their new pastime. They followed the vintage charts and vineyard reports of Europe in the same way they followed the ponies, with pluck and powerful connections. While serving a four-year jail sentence in the Tower of London, the fourth earl of Salisbury kept abreast of the latest vintages by having his wine merchant make deliveries to his cell.

It's not like other countries weren't drinking wine. By the 1600s, the French, Italians, and Germans were downing thirty-two gallons per person per year. But, for them, wine was a homegrown drink that farmers and kings alike could enjoy as opposed to England, where vineyards had not become a part of everyday life. Because of Henry's marriage, wine remained an expensive import that set you *apart* from everyday life, just as the aristocrats intended. Besides, it would only be wasted on the beer-swilling lower classes:

> *"To treat a poor wretch with a bottle of Burgundy . . .*
> *is like giving a pair of laced ruffles to a man that has*
> *never a shirt on his back."* —THOMAS BROWN,
> SEVENTEENTH-CENTURY ENGLISH WRITER

Wine became an official symbol of fancy-pants-ness. By the 1800s, commoners could drink like the posh people by going to taverns that advertised an international selection of wines. Of course, these "international wines" were usually turnip juice and lead oxide fermented in the tavern cellar, but it didn't matter.

The actual wine had become secondary to the *image* of drinking wine, and any indications of poshness were highly sought after. In 1855, France classified its wines by quality. Bordeaux was given top ranking, and within two years, it went from selling 53 million to 133 million cases.

Unbeknownst to the customers, those 1850s Bordeaux were about to become a very wise investment. Because less than a decade later, wine was on the verge of extinction, and it would never taste quite the same again.

Lousy Bug

In 1863, a strange and terrible thing was happening in Provence.

The grapevines were dying. And what was worse, it was beginning to spread. In '67, it happened in Bordeaux, then all of France. In the 1870s, it hit Italy and then Spain.

Grape growers were desperate to stop it. They tried every method from modern (fumigating, which unfortunately killed the vines) to biblical (flooding the fields) to some more old-fashioned voodoo (burying a toad under each vine). Nothing worked. Oddly enough, the same phenomenon had occurred in America for centuries, thwarting every entrepreneur (including Thomas Jefferson) who tried to start a wine industry on the east coast.

> THE BEST USE OF BAD WINE IS TO DRIVE AWAY POOR RELATIONS." —FRENCH PROVERB

It was perplexing because grapevines could and did grow easily. When the Viking Leif the Lucky stumbled onto North America in the year A.D. 1000 he named it "Vineland." Unfortunately, these were a thick, tough-rooted breed of vine that produced grapes too tasteless for wine. But when Europeans arrived, they figured their own wine vines would flourish just as well as the Viking vines.

They didn't. So eventually, frustrated wine makers tried a reverse experiment. They sent samples of American vines to Europe to test the difference in soil. What they didn't know was that they also sent the problem—a tiny, root-eating bug named *Phylloxera vastatrix*, that existed only in the Mississippi River Valley. At least it did, until it hitched a ride with those samples into the vineyards of Europe, where the vines had no natural defenses against its appetite. Phylloxera swept across the continent like a fat man at an all-you-can-eat buffet (for an alternate phylloxera/fat man metaphor, see page 85).

By 1880, phylloxera had snacked its way through 6.25 million acres in France alone. Wine production was down two-thirds and falling fast when someone realized that if the problem came from the west, so might the solution.

Remember those vines Leif the Lucky found? I didn't describe their tough, thick roots for no reason. They'd evolved as a natural defense against phylloxera. Desperate Europeans tried grafting these tougher American roots onto their delicate wine vines, and it worked.

Thus began the tedious process of grafting every vine in Europe onto American roots. Let me repeat that for emphasis. In France alone, *6.25 million acres of vines* had to be grafted *one by one* onto new roots!

Certain remote regions like Chile were unaffected, but 85 percent of vines in the world today are grafted. And phylloxera is such a tenacious little critter that even now, ungrafted vines will die in European soil. This has sparked a lively debate among wine aficionados as to whether wine was better before phylloxera and the introduction of coarse American roots.

The immediate impact of the bug was unquestionable. It caused such a shortfall in production that dishonest distributors began forging labels from high-end regions and watering down their wine. European governments were eventually forced to step in and crack down, but in the meantime the damage was done.

Posh wine critics continued telling people that if they didn't serve specific wines on specific occasions, they would suffer permanent and debilitating social ridicule. Faced with these strict commandments and the fact that many postphylloxera wines were fraudulent, casual drinkers did what was only natural—threw up their hands, turned to less demanding drinks like whiskey, and developed a deep-seated fear of wine.

"WHAT IS MAN, WHEN YOU COME TO THINK UPON HIM, BUT A MINUTELY SET, INGENIOUS MACHINE FOR TURNING WITH INFINITE ARTFULNESS, THE RED WINE OF SHIRAZ INTO URINE?"—ISAK DINESEN

The culture of European wine had backed itself into an insulated and exclusive corner. Fortunately, the New World offered a way out.

Brave New World

Starting in the fifteenth century, the countries of Europe (the Old World) encircled the globe in search of regions to colonize (the New World). And all the usual suspects (missionaries and upper-crust Brits) brought their love of wine with them.

Phylloxera prevented grapes from growing on the east coast of North America, but they grew just fine in Mexico for the sixteenth-century Spanish conquistadors. So well, in fact, that the king of Spain banned commercial wine production for fear that it would hurt the sales of Spanish wine. That left wine, once again, in the enthusiastic hands of the Church. Franciscan priests traveled to South and North America, wining all the way. By the 1700s, California had established twenty-two separate vineyards/missions.

In South Africa, the first vineyard was planted in 1655, by the Dutch governor. But being Dutch, wine was not his forte. South Africa wine began to thrive because of British sailors, who would stop off on their journey to and from India to replenish their officers' vital liquor supplies.

"FROM WINE WHAT SUDDEN FRIENDSHIP SPRINGS!"—JOHN GAY

British officers thought of wine as a civilizing force, which is why they planted Australia's first vineyard in the governor's mansion in 1791. They were promoting wine in an attempt to wean Australians off their more rambunctious tipple, rum, which was starting to cause problems, like, for instance, the toppling of the Australian government (see "Rum Rebellion," page 238).

(see "Rum Rebellion," page 238)

"A BOTTLE OF WINE CONTAINS MORE PHILOSOPHY THAN ALL THE BOOKS IN THE WORLD."
–LOUIS PASTEUR

These New World countries didn't have Europe's centuries of vinicultural tradition, but they offered wine makers the same thing they offered all immigrants, wide open spaces and a chance to rectify the sins of the past.

For instance, the French monks, who knew the minute flavor differences between vineyards, began the practice of naming wines by geographical location. The equivalent would be if Guinness, instead of referring to itself descriptively as "stout," referred to itself as "southwest of Dublin, uphill from the Liffey River, next to the gas station." It was well understood by the cognoscenti that a bottle of Burgundy meant Pinot Noir, but left the amateur drinker in the dark.

The New World had no such luxury. Fledgling wineries had to inform people exactly what their wine tasted like, so they labeled their wine by style (Chardonnay, Merlot, Cabernet, etc.).

Famous geography was Europe's blessing, but also its curse. They didn't have any left. The areas that *could* be cultivated *had* been, intensively. Wineries stayed small because there was no physical room to get larger. This helped maintain quality, but kept prices high. The New World had no such problem, and megawineries were built that could produce a million bottles a day for cheap.

Of course, the quality wasn't so hot at first, but, here again, they weren't hidebound by history. European wine makers considered themselves artists, so they were shocked when New World wineries utilized a concept they considered anathema—technology. In the 1970s, California wine makers began using temperature-controlled fermentation, a technique that beer makers had been using since the sixteenth century (see "Testicle Yeast," page 23).

The result was cleaner, fruitier wine. *Too* fruity, sniffed European wine makers, no complexity. All of which is an accurate description of the *style*, but not of the *quality*, of the wine as the world discovered in 1976. That was the year three French judges, at an international competition in Paris, awarded the top prize, for the first time, to an American wine.

New World wine wasn't just cheap, plentiful, and easily labeled. It was good.

And while the Old World still accounts for 75 percent of the world's wine output (about 7 billion gallons), the New World is slowly closing the gap. And year by year, wine sheds a little more of its historical baggage as the drink of the gods and elite, and can be seen for what it actually is, a glorious act of nature that can be enjoyed by all.

USELESS STUFF

Grape

- The average number of grapes in a bottle of wine: 600.

- The average cost of the grapes that go into a $20 bottle of wine: $2.64.

- The number of wine grape varieties that exist in the world today: 10,000.

- Wine grapes are grown on over 20 million acres of land, making them the number-one fruit crop in the world.

Bottle

- The most expensive bottle of wine ever purchased was a bottle of 1787 Château Lafite that belonged to Thomas Jefferson (his initials were etched onto it). The bottle sold at Christie's in 1985 for £105,000 (about $200,000). Eleven months later, the cork dried out, slipped into the bottle and spoiled the wine, thus making it the world's most expensive bottle of vinegar.

- Punt: Also called the "kick-up." This is the indentation at the bottom of the wine bottle. A natural side effect of glass blowing, it became useful as a trap for sediment.

- Ullage (ul-ij) *n.*: In a bottle of wine, the empty space between the cork and the actual wine. Became a term of abuse in the British Navy to describe a ship's crew as useless. Sample sentence: "Avast, I've seen babies raised faster than that sail, ya wormy-armed chicken-legged ullage."

Vineyard

- The soil of the Clos de Vougeot vineyard in the Burgundy region is considered so precious that vineyard workers are required to scrape it from their shoes before leaving work each day.

- With over 5.5 million visitors a year, Napa Valley has surpassed Disneyland as California's most popular tourist destination.

- The largest wine cellar in the world is near Capetown, South Africa. It covers twenty-five acres and can hold up to 36 million gallons.

Vintage

121 B.C. "Opimion" was the first vintage wine referred to in print. By the time it was rated "of the highest excellence" by the Roman historian Pliny the Elder, it was already two hundred years old.

Butler

Derived from the Old French *bouteillier*, or "bottler." This became the title of the manservant who maintained and monitored the wine cellar. The job was considered so important to a gentleman's lifestyle that the *bouteillier* became the head servant in any household.

One Way to Get Wine Stains Out

Ancient wine was red. White wine only came along in the medieval era. According to legend, the emperor Charlemagne was persuaded to plant white wine grapes throughout his kingdom by his wife, who didn't like the way red wine stained his lovely white beard.

Stomped to Death

The practice of stomping grapes with bare feet to extract the juice may seem quaint and fun, but oddly enough it was a fairly dangerous job. Fermentation releases alcohol and carbon dioxide, so standing in a large tub of fermenting grapes meant you were standing in a rising column of carbon dioxide, which could—and sometimes did—result in suffocation and death.

Winner of the Pretentious Wine Writer's "WHAT did he just say?!" Award

"Red bordeaux is like the lawful wife: an excellent beverage that goes with every dish and enables one to enjoy one's food. But now and then a man wants a change, and champagne is the most complete and exhilarating change . . . it is like a woman of the streets: everyone that can afford it tries it sooner or later, but it has no real attraction. Moselle [a German wine] is like the girl of fourteen to eighteen: light, quick on the tongue, with an exquisite, evanescent perfume, but little body. It may be used constantly and in quantities, but must be taken young."
—FRANK HARRIS, MY LIFE AND LOVES, 1925, APPARENTLY AFTER HAVING A FEW DRINKS AT THE LOCAL PLAYGROUND

USEFUL STUFF

"When it comes to wine, I tell people to throw away the vintage charts and invest in a corkscrew. The best way to learn about wine is the drinking."
—ALEXIS LICHINE, WINE WRITER/MAKER

Serving Temp

White: 50°F. Red: 63°F.

The general wisdom is that white wine should be chilled and red wine should be room temperature. But refrigerators are set much lower than 50°F, and "room temperature" originally referred to rooms in drafty castles. The simplest method is the twenty-minute rule: take a white wine out of the fridge twenty minutes before serving; stick a red wine in the fridge twenty minutes before serving.

Red Wine versus White Wine

All grapes actually produce a pale yellow juice. Red wine is created by allowing the juice to remain in contact with the grape skins and stems throughout the fermentation process. They contribute one of red wine's most important flavor components, tannin, which is what makes your mouth pucker when you taste a dry red (and, unfortunately, is what causes red wine headaches). For white wines, the skin is removed before fermentation.

Storing

"I made wine out of raisins so I wouldn't have to wait for it to age." —STEVEN WRIGHT

If you don't finish an open bottle of wine, stick it in the fridge. Wines last six to sixteen times longer in the refrigerator than if they're allowed to sit around at room temperature. For similar reasons, if you're storing bottles, keep it in a cool (50 to 60°F), dark place. Light spoils wine, which is why most bottles are tinted.

TASTING CHEAT SHEET

Considering there are entire books devoted to wine tasting, it's pointless to go too in-depth. But here's a basic flavor summary of the major types of grapes/wines:

White

CHARDONNAY: Far and away the most popular white because of the grape's ability to grow well on any type of soil. Its flavor is compatible with oak, so almost every Chardonnay is barrel-aged. Flavors: vanilla, toffee, butterscotch, apple, and pineapple.

RIESLING: Normally associated with Germany and thus thought of as a sweet wine, but it can be dry as well. Look for the word *trocken*, or dry, on the label. Flavors: floral, apricot, and honey.

SAUVIGNON BLANC: The crisp, dry, light-bodied white wine. Flavors: herbs, mown grass, minerals.

PINOT GRIGIO: Also known as Pinot Gris. Mellow, full-bodied, with low acidity. Flavor: skins of fruit (orange peel, peach skin).

Red

CABERNET SAUVIGNON: Like Chardonnay, this grape is popular because it grows well everywhere, resulting in good bargains. Dry (high tannins) and dark. Flavors: black currant, chocolate, toast.

MERLOT: Popular because of its low tannins and its high quality at a young age. Flavors: very fruity, floral (rose petals), tea leaves.

PINOT NOIR: Highly prized by wine aficionados because it only grows in very particular regions and has complex taste. Flavors: red berry fruits, earthy or woodsy.

SHIRAZ: Not as popular for casual drinking because of its dry, challenging taste. Flavors: spices (black pepper), smoked meat, lead pencil (hey, I don't come up with these).

ZINFINDEL: The most-grown red in California. Tends to be very dark and dry. Flavors: berries, spicy.

A Good Wine Word to Learn
(Plus! A Brief History of Economics)

TERROIR: The fantastically romantic French concept that a wine's flavor is the combination of sun,
shade, soil, and rain produced by an individual plot of
land. The idea being that you're not just drinking
wine, you're drinking the geography that created it.

Terroir is simply one expression of wine's unique
trait of tasting different from location to location. The
ancient Egyptians noticed this attribute and began
buying wine from locations all along the Nile, consti-
tuting the first real trade between the otherwise self-
sufficient Egyptian farming communities. This trading
required the creation of concepts such as market
prices, common currency, and contracts, so these first
rumblings of *terroir* appreciation were, according to
many historians, the probable basis of all economics.

Humphrey Bogart

(1899–1957)

He was a brooding, craggy-faced, funny-looking shrimp, but when he had a drink in one hand and a gun in the other, the cameras *loved* Humphrey Bogart.

The son of a prominent New York surgeon, he was groomed from an early age for a life of medicine. Bogart attended the hoity-toity prep school Phillips Academy in Andover, Massachusetts, but he soon rebelled, got expelled, and joined the navy to fight in World War I.

After the war, he moved back to New York with an interest in the stage. Things didn't go well at first, but after a number of lean years, he got his big break playing a psychotic villain in the hit play and film *The Petrified Forest*. This quickly led to a string of other gangster-villain roles.

Bogart's star was on the rise, but his personal life was still in the drunk tank. He was already on his third marriage, and the unhappy, heavy-drinking couple became known as the "Battling Bogarts." Plates and potted plants got smashed in every Hollywood nightclub they went to. And they went to a lot. Bogie acquired a weathered, whiskey-beaten appearance that landed him his first leading role as the hard-boiled detective Sam Spade, in *The Maltese Falcon*.

The film was a hit and Bogie went from two-bit villain to romantic leading man, on-screen and off. On the set of *To Have and Have Not*, his costar was a nineteen-year-old ingenue named Lauren Bacall, and she quickly became his fourth and final wife.

The happy newlyweds moved to a mansion in Holmby Hills and hosted innumerable late-night parties. An ad hoc drinking club soon formed, including Frank Sinatra, Judy Garland, Spencer Tracy, Swifty Lazar, and a gang of other Hollywood sorts. And on one particularly debauched night, Bacall immortalized them all when she quipped that they looked "like a goddamned rat pack."

The Holmby Hills Rat Pack was born. It eventually ran its course, but one member of the group decided to keep the party going. Frank Sinatra formed his own, more famous Rat Pack with Dean Martin and Sammy Davis Jr.

Throughout his career, Bogart's biggest on-screen costars were a bottle and a cigarette. In the end, it was the cigarettes that killed him. He died of throat cancer in 1957, with Lauren Bacall by his side.

> *"The whole world is about three drinks behind."*

> *"People who don't drink are afraid of revealing themselves."*

> *"What do you do with a kid? They don't drink."* —ON HIS IMPENDING FATHERHOOD

> *"I should never have switched from Scotch to martinis."*
> —REPUTED TO BE HIS DYING WORDS

CHAMPAGNE

BORN TO LIVE THE HIGH LIFE

"Come quickly, I am tasting stars!"
—DOM PÉRIGNON, UPON TASTING HIS FIRST
CHAMPAGNE

Take a tour of any champagne vineyard and you'll hear the legend of how a Benedictine monk named Dom Pierre Pérignon burst out with that spiffy little bon mot when he invented champagne by accident one day.

This is a great story, and you hate to take anything away from the guy (since not only was he a monk, he was also blind); unfortunately, it's only half-true. He *might* have said it, and there's a reason his name is synonymous with champagne, but like almost all things related to alcohol, things only *really* got moving once the British took an interest.

Let's start at the beginning.

Champagne is actually the name of the northern most grape-growing region of France, and ever since Roman times, it's produced a peculiar sort of wine. It was a basic nonbubbly "still" wine back then, but the colder, northern weather gave the grapes (and wine) a sharp, distinctive flavor that was quite popular.

But there was a problem.

Devil Wine

Turning grapes into wine requires fermentation. The fermentation process occurs when yeast feeds on sugar. This produces two by-products: alcohol and CO_2 gas. The catch is, the process only works in a warm environment.

The colder, northern weather in Champagne created a shorter growing season, which meant that by the time the grapes were picked and pressed and ready to ferment, the first winter frost would roll in and stop the fermentation halfway. Unaware of this, the monks would transfer the wine from barrels into bottles over the course of winter, so when the warmer weather returned in spring, fermentation would start back up again—inside the bottles.

Wine became fizzy; bottles exploded in the cellars and flying glass gouged out eyeballs. Monks working in the wine cellars were forced to wear iron masks. Before it was coveted as "champagne," the French had other names for it—"cork-popper" and "devil wine." They were *not* happy with bubbles in their wine, and worked furiously (and unsuccessfully) to eliminate them.

"PLEASURE WITHOUT CHAMPAGNE IS PURELY ARTIFICIAL."
—OSCAR WILDE

Meanwhile, the British had taken a liking to this white wine from Champagne, bubbles included. And never a people to be easily deterred from a good drink, the Brits hammered out a few inventions to keep their bottles from exploding. Instead of trying to change the wine, they simply changed the packaging.

ALCOHOLICA ESOTERICA

They created stronger bottles that could withstand the pressure building up from the gas. And while the French were using wooden plugs in their bottles, the Brits used corks to seal the air in.

In 1662, thirty years before Dom Pérignon began seeing stars, the writer Christopher Merrit noted that "wine coopers of recent times use vast quantities of sugar and molasses to make them [sic] drink brisk and sparkling." In other words, they liked a bit of brisk and sparkle in their wine *so* much, they were actually creating *more* bubbles.

Thus, the British were responsible for the bottle, the stopper, and the method that created wine with bubbles. But it was Pérignon who transformed it from ordinary wine-with-a-bit-of-fizz into champagne.

A Monk and His Bubbles

In 1688, when Dom Pérignon became the cellar master of the Abbey of Hautvillers, he decided to work *with* the bubbles rather than against them. He imported the strong new bottles and airtight corks from England and began creating a radically new wine that was more than the sum of all these parts.

First, he invented a gentler grape press, which was then placed out in the fields near the vines. By pressing the grapes immediately, no juice would be lost during a lengthy transit back to the winery. He also created a new range of flavors by the heretical practice of blending several different types of still wine together. After that, all he had to do was throw some yeast into the bottle to start the second, carbonating fermentation, stick a cork in, and *voilà*!

The first bottle of bubbly as we know it today was uncorked in 1690.

"Money and champagne always find each other."
—WILLIAM GRIMES, *STRAIGHT UP OR ON THE ROCKS*

So how did an interesting little invention by a blind monk in a cellar out in the French countryside become the drink of kings?

Well, it didn't happen right away. Champagne was expensive to make. Plus, it ran into trouble with the law. At the time, regulations forbade the transportation of bottled wine. And champagne, by its very nature, can't travel in barrels. So it was relatively scarce until the law was struck down in 1728. After that, champagne houses like Taittinger, Moët, Heidsieck, and Clicquot began bubbling up all over the region.

"CHAMPAGNE SHOULD BE COLD, DRY AND, HOPEFULLY, FREE."
—Christian Pol Roger

The champagne boom was under way, and just in time. There was some *serious* partying going on at the royal palace in Versailles.

Those Frolicking French

In 1715, King Louis XIV died when little Louis XV was only five years old. The court, as a mature and reasoning body charged with the awesome task of running the country in the interim, acted as expected. . . . It threw a decades-long houseparty—lavish balls, lascivious quadrille-dancing, powdered fops experimenting with sexual identities, and so forth, all of which ended only when the peasants figured out how to use a guillotine.

In this decadent atmosphere, what better way to show off than by drinking this new-fangled wine that was so expensive and scarce only the wealthiest could obtain a bottle? On top of that, with the court in a randy mood, women were able to broker increasing amounts of power behind the scenes by holding men captive to their . . . umm . . . "charms." A group of mistresses known as *"Les Grande Horizontales"* began to greatly influence the decisions and culture of the court. And champagne was a *big* hit with the horizontal ladies.

> *"Champagne is the only wine that leaves a woman beautiful after drinking it."* —MADAME DE POMPADOUR, OFFICIAL ROYAL MISTRESS TO KING LOUIS XV, 1745–1750

By the time Louis XV was old enough to have an official mistress, champagne had become the semiofficial drink of Versailles. And the new king didn't seem to mind. In fact, Madame de Pompadour made sure to stash two hundred bottles of the stuff in her cellar whenever he paid a visit.

All of this was fine and dandy if you were royalty and had a good wine steward, but otherwise you were out of luck, because despite its new popularity, champagne was still a major headache to drink. Literally. Remember how Pérignon created the fizz by throwing a handful of yeast into the bottle? Well, the yeast didn't go away. It stayed there, and unless the bottle was poured ever so carefully, it clouded up the drink and caused blinding hangovers.

In this case, the adage that the only true cure for a hangover is death proved true. It all ended when a man named François Clicquot died.

The Widow's Good Works

François left the management of his small champagne house to his wife, Nicole Barbe Clicquot, who thereafter became known as the Widow Clicquot (a name more widely recognized in its original French, "Veuve Clicquot").

A widow at twenty-seven, she suddenly had a lot of time and a lot of champagne to tinker with. She quickly built the Clicquot house into an empire and, in her spare time, invented pink champagne, the now familiar mushroom cork, and most importantly, in 1816, she created "riddling."

This entailed turning the bottles upside down, over the course of many weeks, until the yeast was in the neck, where it would come out easily when she popped the cork. Then, she simply stuck a new cork in and suddenly had a sludge-free, sparkling-clear bottle. Champagne was now a drink you could chug with abandon.

Which the French royalty did. In fact, they were having such a rip-roaring good time that it wasn't long before their neighbors wanted in on the fun. But it took a little encouragement at first.

"HERE'S TO CHAMPAGNE, THE DRINK DIVINE
THAT MAKES US FORGET OUR TROUBLES;
IT'S MADE OF A DOLLAR'S WORTH OF WINE
AND THREE DOLLARS' WORTH OF BUBBLES."

—ANONYMOUS

Champagne Pop

If you think today's hip-hop rivalries and Courvoisier product placements are anything new under the sun, listen to this:

In 1866, a Victorian music hall singer named George Leybourne rechristened himself "Champagne Charlie," and became the first of the "swells." These were well-dressed, good-looking dandies who wowed poverty-stricken English audiences with songs about their conspicuous consumption and high-flying lifestyle. The craze began with Charlie's first hit:

"A noise all night, in bed all day, and swimming in
Champagne
For Champagne Charlie is my name, Champagne
Charlie is my name.
Some epicures like Burgundy, Hock, Claret, and
Moselle,
But Moët's Vintage only satisfies this Champagne swell;
What matter if to bed I go, and head is muddled thick,
A bottle in the morning sets me right then very quick."

To further this image, Charlie's manager gave him a top-of-the-line four-horse carriage and had him under strict orders to drink nothing but champagne in public. Overnight, Champagne Charlie became a major sex symbol, and his drink of choice became the toast of London.

The makers at Moët, realizing what a PR gold mine this was, commissioned Charlie in 1871 to sing a hit sequel called, somewhat unimaginatively, "Moët and Chandon":

"Champagne Charlie was my name,
Champagne drinking gain'd my fame,
So as of old, when on the spree,
Moët and Chandon's the wine for me."

Of course, where there's room for one sex symbol, there's room for more. Champagne Charlie's chief rival was "The Great Vance." In 1870, Vance made walking at the zoo all the rage (no, seriously) with his aptly titled song, "Walking at the Zoo (Is the OK Thing to Do)."

The Great Vance was no stranger to plugging merchandise: he got his suits for free after singing about his tailor. So he hopped on the bandwagon with his own champagne-endorsement song: "Clicquot." Charlie responded with another wine endorsement and song, and so it went. The two dueled back and forth, singing the praises of any vineyard or brewery that was willing to sponsor them until, quite literally, they ran out of drinks to sing about. And ran themselves into the ground.

Their bad-boy lifestyle took its toll. The Great Vance collapsed and died onstage in 1889. Charlie's lifetime supply of free Moët didn't help him any, either—he died of alcoholism in 1884, at the age of forty-two.

But their work was done; the celebrity endorsement was born. In 1844, 7 million bottles of champagne were sold. By 1899, it was up to 28 million. Champagne had arrived, in style.

Riots and Regulations

"Champagne or Death!" —A PROTEST SLOGAN DURING THE 1911 CHAMPAGNE RIOTS

With champagne such a hot commodity, other grape-growing countries got in on the act. Spain, Italy, Germany, America, and Australia began to create their own champagne. But the locals of Champagne had a head start on the world in terms of name recognition and product, and they meant to keep it. They became incredibly touchy and . . . well . . . *French* about protecting the name, the quality of the drink, and the physical region of Champagne itself.

They secured laws stating that any sparkling wine that isn't from the Champagne region of France cannot be called champagne. All other products must be called sparkling wine. Thus, the land and a winery's right to the champagne name became an incredibly hot commodity.

"I LOVE CHAMPAGNE BECAUSE IT ALWAYS TASTES AS THOUGH MY FOOT'S ASLEEP."
—ART BUCHWALD

In fact, when officials tried redrawing the borders of the region, it sparked off the Champagne Riots of 1908 and 1911. Locals burned the cellars of offending wineries that were suspected of blending foreign, non-Champagne wine into their bubbly. They tore up roads that were used to bring in foreign grapes. The government relented and kept the borders as they were.

The name may be taken, but the ideas of Dom Pérignon and the Widow Clicquot live on. Wineries today still use their basic *méthode champagnoise* to produce fantastic sparkling wines in every corner of the world. Even so, it's the premium French stuff that has a mystique all its own.

It might be a quirk of history, good brand management, or maybe we just really like the bubbles, but the name "champagne" conjures up an alchemy of images—money, success, power, and pleasure—that have become synonymous with *la dolce vita*. And whether it's the music hall swells of yesterday or the hip-hop stars of today, there will always be people willing to sing the praises of living the high life.

USELESS INFO

Under Pressure

The air in a car's tire exerts a pressure of about 30 pounds per square inch (psi). The gas inside a bottle of champagne exerts three times that with 90 psi.

A Whole Lotta Bubbles

Scientists with *way* too much time on their hands have actually created a formula to measure how many bubbles there are in a standard 750-ml bottle of champagne. Answer: Between 44 and 57 *million* bubbles.

Champagne Charlie/Rap Star Redux

In a case of history repeating itself, marketing surveys show that attendees of R and B, rap, or hip-hop concerts are 94 percent more likely than the average person to drink champagne.

Fun Cork Facts

- By the law of averages you are more likely to be killed by a flying champagne cork than by a poisonous spider.

- The speed of a popped champagne cork ranges between thirty-five and one hundred miles per hour.

"THERE ARE TWO CHAMPAGNES ONE CAN'T REFUSE: DOM PÉRIGNON AND THE EVEN SUPERIOR CRISTAL, WHICH IS BOTTLED IN A NATURAL-COLOURED GLASS THAT DISPLAYS ITS PALE BLAZE, A CHILLED FIRE OF SUCH PRICKLY DRYNESS THAT, SWALLOWED, SEEMS NOT TO HAVE BEEN SWALLOWED AT ALL, BUT INSTEAD TO HAVE BEEN TURNED TO VAPOURS ON THE TONGUE, AND BURNED THERE TO ONE SWEET ASH."—TRUMAN CAPOTE

- The world distance record for a cork popped out of a chilled bottle is 177 feet 9 inches, or about two-thirds of a New York City block.

Dandy Facts

- After defeating Napoleon, the British banished him to the island of Saint Helena. To further the punishment, Napoleon was only allowed one bottle of champagne per day. This was clearly too barbarous for English nobleman Sir Walter Scott, who protested that it was cruel to deny the fallen Frenchman the "solace of intoxication."

- Frederick the Great, king of Prussia (1740–1786), disliked the effect of coffee and banned its use by commoners. He himself, however, drank seven to eight cups every morning. Only he preferred making his coffee with champagne rather than hot water.

- High-society dandies in nineteenth-century England insisted that the only way to properly polish boots was with champagne.

Urban Legends that you've probably never heard of but now that you have, they're way too cool to want to debunk them completely

There is a legend that the traditional, wide-brimmed, shallow champagne glass (the "coupe") was modeled upon Marie Antoinette's breasts. While this isn't *exactly* true (the design first appeared for sparkling wine in England in 1663), she *did* use her breast as a model for four glasses to give to the champagne-loving king.

However, experts believe the shallow design of the coupe allows too much fizz to escape. They prefer the flute-shaped glass. Sadly, there is no research indicating who's anatomical parts *that* design might be based on.

―――

It's rumored (and not denied by biographers) that Marilyn Monroe once took a bubble bath in a tub filled with 350 bottles of champagne.

> I only drink Champagne when I'm happy, and when I'm sad. Sometimes I drink it when I'm alone. When I have company I consider it obligatory. I trifle with it if I am not hungry and drink it when I am. Otherwise, I never touch it—unless I'm thirsty."—MADAME LILY BOLLINGER

Why There's Foil on the Bottle

In the old days, the foil was lead-lined and ostensibly used to keep mice from nibbling at the corks; however, there was an earlier, thriftier reason for this tradition. When Madame Clicquot invented the idea of opening bottles and pouring the yeast out, no one could control exactly how much liquid foamed out with it. The foil was used to hide the fact that all bottles contained wildly varying levels of champagne. This practice only stopped when the British complained about getting ripped off. After that, all bottles were topped off to a set level.

A Neat Bar Trick

A raisin dropped in a glass of fresh champagne will continually circulate from the bottom of the glass to the top and back again.

Geeky Explanation of Neat Bar Trick

Bubbles form on the wrinkles, lifting the raisin up like a hot-air balloon. Then, when it rises to the surface, the bubbles burst and it falls back down again. Depending on how much you've had to drink, you can ascribe various metaphors to the raisin: Icarus, Sisyphus, the Third Reich, the Roman empire, Shelley Long's career, etc.

The Glass Pyramid

To build a pyramid of champagne glasses for a champagne cascade, the following ratio is considered best:

Base level = 60 glasses
first level = 30
second level = 10
third level = 4
fourth level = 1

USEFUL INFO

The Lay of the Land

The Champagne region, for all its importance, is only around 75,000 acres. This is just 2.5 percent of all vineyards in France. But despite its small size, Champagne produces 10 percent of the world's total output of sparkling wine.

Champagne's Grapes

While each house creates a slightly different blend for their various brands, Champagne is basically comprised of three grape varieties. French law requires that each vineyard grows their grapes in this ratio: 37 percent Pinot Noir, 37 percent Pinot Meunier, and 26 percent Chardonnay.

A Hundred Wines in One

The blenders for each champagne house are artists in their own right. Between one hundred and two hundred different wines might be blended to create one single base wine (the first stage of champagne). The grapes for one bottle will sometimes come from thirty or forty different villages.

How to Rate Champagne

A scoring system is used to rate the quality of a champagne in several categories: On the Eye, On the Nose, On the Palate. These are the basic categories used to rate any alcohol, but that implies that champagne is just another ordinary drink, which clearly won't do. Thus, it is also rated for Gastronomy and Imagination.

Imagination is broken down into four categories—Body, Spirit, Soul, and Heart—which is then *further* subdivided into these categories (and I'm not making this up): Charm, Sensuality, Passion, Ecstasy, Mystery, Intelligence, Enthusiasm, Marriage, and Tenderness.

"ALAS, I AM DYING BEYOND MY MEANS."
—OSCAR WILDE, AS HE SIPPED CHAMPAGNE ON HIS DEATHBED

Bubble size is a good indicator of quality. Topflight sparkling wine has tiny bubbles that float upward in a constant stream from the bottom of the glass. Larger bubbles that appear at random are a mark of inferiority. In fact, the French consider big bubbles so odious, so utterly contemptible, they call them *yeux de crapaud,* or "toad's eyes."

Reading the Label

The sweetness of the champagne is always indicated as follows:

- Extra Brut, Brut Nature, or Brut Sauvage: bone dry.

- Brut: very dry.

- Extra Dry: medium dry.

- Sec: slightly sweet.

- Demi-sec: sweet.

- Doux: sweetest.

The label will also indicate which type of champagne it is. Here are the distinctions and what they mean:

NONVINTAGE: Nonvintage is indicated by the lack of a specific year on the label. This means that the bottle was made with a blend of wines from several different years.

VINTAGE: A vintage year occurs only four or five times every ten years. This means that the grapes from that single year were of sufficient quantity and quality to create the champagne blend. In addition, vintage bottles tend to be aged several years longer than nonvintage.

"PRESTIGE" CUVÉE: A cuvée is always from a vintage year, and uses only the first pressing of the best grapes for its blend. A cuvée also has much longer aging requirements than either vintage or nonvintage.

There is always a much smaller quantity of cuvée produced, and coupled with its high demand, it tends to
be exorbitantly priced. In general, the taste difference
between a good vintage champagne and a good cuvée
is not enough to justify the massive price differential.
Leave it for the really discerning connoisseurs and the
dip-shits trying to show off in front of strippers.

Serving Temp

Champagne people tend to be even touchier on this
issue than wine people and basically treat every bottle
as if it were the baby Jesus himself. So once you've
read this, don't say I didn't warn you.

For maximum taste and bubbliness, champagne
should be served at around 45°F (7° to 8°C). Note:
Most refrigerators are around 37°F.

Champagne should never be left in the refrigerator for more than a couple days. The chill flattens the
taste, and the vibrations from the motor hurt the carbonation (see what I mean?). The best method is to
stick the bottle into the fridge about two hours before
serving, or by putting it into a bucket of half ice/half
water. Throwing a handful of salt into the bucket will
reduce its temperature below zero and help the chill-
ing process.

How to Avoid Your Champagne Going Flat

You and your significant other have gone through two-thirds of a bottle. Barry White is on the stereo. You slip away to the boudoir to explore your mutual feelings in a tender, caring manner, and also, to do the nasty. But when you come back a few hours later, the champagne is flat, the magic has evaporated, and your lover leaves you for someone classier, someone who can keep their bubbles bubbling. There are two ways to avoid this cruel fate:

1. You can buy an inexpensive, plastic champagne stopper at a wine store, *or* you can use

2. *The Spoon Trick:* Now, I know I'll be accused of spreading an old wives' tale, but the fact is, I've experimented with this under strict scientific conditions (downing several bottles in one sitting, but making notations on a clipboard and, at all times, wearing safety goggles) and for whatever reason, it works. Simply take a normal metal kitchen spoon and stick it handle first into the neck of the bottle. The round part of the spoon will stick out of the neck, and, again, I have no clue how this works, but your champagne will stay bubbly for many hours.

Opening the Bottle

It's actually very easy. Avoid the locker room victory shower technique of wiggling the cork back and forth with your thumbs. To open the bottle, simply hold the cork firmly and twist. You should feel the pressure inside the bottle pushing the cork out as you do this. Just remember the advice from one of those roaring, black-and-white William Powell movies: "It shouldn't pop. It should cough, apologetically."

DISTILLED SPIRITS

THE "STILL" IN DISTILLED SPIRITS

One of history's great ironies is that liquor owes its existence to the Arab world, where religion strictly forbids alcohol.

Distillation is the simple boiling of a substance to separate out the water and create a more concentrated product. The still that performs this operation was invented in China, India, or Greece (take your pick), but it was the Middle East where the concept was preserved and perfected as Arab alchemists used it to create perfumes and medicine. When the Muslim Moors invaded southern Europe in A.D. 711, alchemists tried distilling the local wine into medicine. What they got was brandy and a brand-new Arabic word, "alcohol."

Al-koh'l originally referred to a black powder used as eye makeup. It later became a general term for any distilled powder or essence. Our meaning for "alcohol" descends from the Arabic phrase *"al-koh'l* of wine," meaning the "essence of wine."

Before the Moors, Europe had been a wine and beer continent, but the gospel of the still spread quickly as Europeans marveled at its ability to transform any region's local staple into a high-octane spirit—potatoes into vodka, barley into whiskey, sugar into rum.

As you read the histories of these spirits, you'll notice a pattern emerging. They all start out as caustic, throat-burning brews, but then make a sudden leap in quality, respectability, and commercial potential. A lot of that is due to the invention of the Coffey still in 1830.

Aeneas Coffey was an Irish excise officer (see "Curst Horse Leeches," page 83) in charge of confiscating illegal stills. In the course of his job, he came across the design for an ingenious still that could more efficiently create beer. Coffey essentially took the same design, replaced the word "beer" with "hard liquor" and patented it under his own name. It was able to process alcohol so quickly and inexpensively that it enabled the creation of large-scale, global-minded distilleries, whose stills can rise up to four stories high.

Here's a general rule: If it's light and less flavorful (vodka, gin, light rum), it's made in a Coffey still. But if it's dark (brandy, Scotch, dark rum), modern distillers still swear by the rich flavors created in the slow, inefficient, centuries-old pot stills.

WHISKEY

THE OFFICIAL BEVERAGE OF REBEL NATIONS

SCOTCH

The Age of Legends

The exact origins of whiskey are mysterious, since they lie in the ancient realm of the Celts, who were much more into being muddy and killing each other than into keeping accurate records. Legend has it that Saint Patrick brought the art of distilling to Ireland in the fifth century, but this is somewhat suspect since the same legend also insists that he drove the snakes out of Ireland. (Note: If that isn't a metaphor for detox, this author doesn't know *what* is.) As for how whiskey made it over to Scotland, well, here again legend steps in to explain that an Irish giant leaped the channel with a cask of whiskey on his back and showed the Scottish how to make it.

The slightly less sexy explanation is that eleventh- or twelfth-century European monks traveled to both places carrying the word of God (Christianity) and distilling the "water of life" (*Uisge beatha* in Gaelic). But Scottish whiskey finally stepped out of myth and into reality in 1494, when it was mentioned in print by the king's bookkeeper: "4 bolls of malt to Friar John Cor wherewith to make aqua vitae."

Admittedly, an accountant's receipt isn't the most thrilling of literary debuts, but it illustrates a couple of interesting points: four bolls of malt is enough for fifteen hundred bottles. Clearly, whiskey was popular long before 1494. More importantly, it shows that whiskey making was still the exclusive domain of friars and monasteries.

But all that was about to change, because the king of England had lovin' on his mind.

> "THE LIGHT MUSIC OF WHISKEY
> FALLING INTO A GLASS—
> AN AGREEABLE INTERLUDE."
> —JAMES JOYCE

Salt of the Earth

Henry VIII was bored with his wife and he wanted to trade her in for a younger model, but the pope refused to grant a divorce. Henry didn't want any part of a religion that kept him from his sovereign right to sleep with a younger woman, so in the 1530s, he formed his very own Church of England. Not so coincidentally, this also gave him an excuse to seize the Catholic Church's land holdings throughout Britain. Monasteries were shut and monks were fired.

What do you do when you're an unemployed monk? You market your other talent, which for Scottish monks was making whiskey. So while Henry was whittling off his wives' heads, whiskey stills began springing up in every village and every farm in Scotland.

Because for farmers, whiskey was the best thing to come along since sheep-sex.

Never an easy life, farming was even more difficult back then. Grain crops were too bulky to transport to market, but they couldn't be stored since the damp weather caused mold and rot to set in almost immediately.

> "A TORCHLIGHT PROCESSION MARCHING DOWN YOUR THROAT."—JOHN O'SULLIVAN, AMERICAN JOURNALIST

Distilling solved all these problems at once. A whole field of grain could be reduced into a few profitable, easily carried jugs. And farming didn't seem like such a hard life after a few *skalks,* an early-morning drink of whiskey that translates literally as "a sharp blow to the head." Barley, long thought to be an inferior food crop, became known as the "drink crop," and up to one-third of farmland was soon devoted to it.

In fact, distilling barley became so popular that when a crop failure hit Scotland in 1597, the government had to ban it to ensure there would be enough grain left for eating. The government tried regulating whiskey several times, but the farmers never paid much mind to the laws issuing forth from the big cities. They kept right on drinking what they wanted.

The Scottish had a testy relationship at best with their government, which was under the control of a cruel and foreign land—England. In the 1600s, James VI decided to "bring the Highlands and Isles to civility," and by any means necessary. Scottish clan chieftains were kidnapped and forced to send their children to English schools. Gaelic language and customs were banned. Except for whiskey.

It was certainly a custom; it was practically a way of

life. "They continued drinking sometimes twenty-four, sometimes forty-eight hours. It was reckoned a piece of manhood to drink until they became drunk, and there were two men with a [wheel]barrow attending punctually on such occasions," was how the Scottish islands were described in 1695. But the reason the English didn't ban whiskey was simple—they wanted in on the action.

When England incorporated Scotland into the United Kingdom in 1707, it decided to finance the endeavor with a tax on whiskey. England had no idea of the headache it was in for.

Smuggler's Paradise

"Freedom an' whisky gang thegither!"
—ROBERT BURNS

Imagine it from the Scottish point of view.

You're a poor, Gaelic-speaking farmer. You grow your own food, but the only thing that earns your actual rent money is distilling *uisge beatha*. Suddenly, a bunch of foreigners ride into your village demanding taxes on something their English tongues can't even pronounce (they call it "whiskey"). Plus, those taxes finance the occupying army that's been stomping on your country for years.

Suddenly, whiskey wasn't just a drink, it was a form of patriotism.

"IT REKINDLES OLD FIRES IN US, OUR HATRED OF CANT AND PRIVILEGE, OUR CONVIVIALITY, OUR SENSE OF MANHOOD, AND ABOVE ALL, OUR LOVE OF SCOTLAND."
—SIR ROBERT LOCKHART

Distilling, smuggling, and drinking whiskey became the Scottish way of sticking it to The Man. And, as luck would have it, God himself couldn't have designed a better smuggler's paradise than the mountainous Highlands of Scotland. If a band of tax men arrived in a village, locals would send up flags or chimney smoke to warn the distillers in the hills. Signals would then go up from one hilltop to the next and a whole mountain range worth of stills could vanish before the raiding party even began.

"I GOT RID OF ALL THOSE REPORTERS."

"WHAT DID YOU TELL THEM?"

"WE'RE OUT OF SCOTCH."

"WHAT A GRUESOME IDEA."

—MYRNA LOY AND WILLIAM POWELL,
ANOTHER THIN MAN

Smuggling became a vastly creative and communal affair. In 1723, the head of customs reported, "If our officers happen to see any running goods, they are immediately mobbed and the goods carried off by persons in women's habits." And sometimes, there were even women in those clothes. Scotland's "women of spirit" wore voluminous skirts to conceal containers of whiskey underneath. Young women strapped on two-gallon belly canteens, which simulated a pregnant stomach. Priests allowed barrels to be hidden under their church pulpits and blessed empty coffins used as transport.

Even the animal kingdom joined in. Dogs were trained to make solo treks over mountain paths while carrying pigs bladders of whiskey. Yearly cattle drives to market became vastly more profitable when the herds concealed hundreds of casks strapped to their bellies.

The incentives for smuggling only increased as the union with Scotland introduced the English to this northern drink. Commercial distilleries were built to meet the rising demand, but the public wasn't interested in this mass-produced product. It preferred the carefully tended, small-batch whiskeys made in the hills. Moreover, the legal distilleries just couldn't compete with the sheer volume of illicit whiskey.

Moonshiners were making ten times the amount of legal distilleries in the 1700s. The town of Edinburgh, for instance, had eight legal distilleries, and over four hundred illegal ones. But that was peanuts compared to the Highlands, where between 1816 and 1820, fourteen thousand illegal stills were discovered!

A cycle developed: England would tax whiskey, so smuggling would increase, cutting into England's profits, inspiring a further increase in taxes, which in turn increased smuggling, and so on.

Nothing the English did seemed to help. When they raised taxes in 1725, riots broke out in Edinburgh and Glasgow. These were quelled in bloody fashion, but to ensure even swifter troop movements for future riots, the army built hundreds of roads and bridges along the borders of Scotland . . . which the smugglers immediately used to expedite their deliveries.

By the 1800s, the border town of Carlisle estimated that eight to eleven thousand gallons of whiskey *a week* were passing through. There was a flood of whiskey racing over Scotland, and the only ones standing against the deluge were a hapless bunch known as excise officers.

Curst Horse Leeches

Tax men. "Gaugers," the Scottish called them. The excise officers were hopelessly understaffed, outclassed, and overwhelmed as they tried to police an entire nation that hated their guts. Their situation was best summed up by Scotland's national poet, Robert Burns, who described them as "curst horse leeches" right before money problems forced him to take a job as one of them. Morale was clearly not so hot.

It didn't help that their efforts were, for the most part, pointless. If they made an arrest, the moonshiners stood trial before local judges who got on the bench by dint of being rich landowners. And the way landowners got rich was by selling their crops to moonshiners. Convictions were infrequent. But when they did happen, local wardens were more than sympathetic. Some prisoners were even allowed out at night to tend their stills so long as they returned for lockup the next morning with a jar of whiskey for the guards.

The whole farce reached its climax with King George IV's visit to Scotland in 1822. During the free-flowing festivities, he singled out whiskey from the town of Glenlivet as his favorite. In fact, he ordered that Glenlivet be used for toasts at all official Scottish ceremonies. The town of Glenlivet, of course, did not have a single legal distillery in it. It did have two hundred illegal ones, though.

The king warmed toward Scotland immensely. He lifted the ban on Gaelic customs and, in 1823, a sensible approach to taxation was worked out. Moonshiners quickly gave way to small, legal distilleries. Whiskey was now legit.

But it was still basically a local drink. It had been associated with smugglers for so long that respectable Brits wouldn't go near it. So how did Scotland emerge as the standard-bearer of all things whiskey? There was plenty of competition. America had a thriving, century-old bourbon industry by then. And Ireland invented the stuff, for God's sake. So why is it that whiskey always seems to taste better when you're wearing a kilt?

The answer is, and I swear I haven't been sniffing glue while writing this, a frumpy queen, a hungry bug, and a hatchet-wielding American.

Frumpy Queen, Hungry Bug

If nothing else, going legit improved whiskey's taste. When it was moonshine, whiskey only aged for the length of time it took to get from the still into your stomach. The 1820s marked the first time whiskey was aged in barrels.

So it tasted respectably good by the time frumpy Queen Victoria took her first tour of Scotland in 1848. She fell in love with the rugged Highlands, where she could escape the stuffy court life and indulge in earthier pursuits like hunting, sleeping with her stable boy, and Scotch.

She ordered all royal coaches to store a bottle beneath the driver's seat in case of emergencies. And she hosted hunts in which every guest was given an entire bottle in the morning to lubricate the trigger finger. Remarkably, most of these guests survived. And when they returned to London, they introduced the rest of high society to the queen's new drink.

To capitalize on this sudden interest, some distillers decided to tailor their drink to the weaker constitutions of these non-Scottish types. In the 1850s, they began blending their malt whiskey with the lighter grain alcohol that was being produced by the latest invention, the Coffey still (see page 77).

> "WHISKEY IS MERELY LEGAL, THOUGH SOME PEOPLE SEEM TO THINK IT'S COMPULSORY."
> —ANONYMOUS

Sales of blended Scottish whiskey took off. The Irish refused to blend and their whiskey, which before then was outselling Scotch three to one, got buried. The Scots had barely finished dancing on the grave of Irish whiskey when a fresh grave was being prepared— brandy had caught a fatal bug.

Its name was phylloxera. And in the 1860s, this vine louse hitched a ride on a boat from the United States and traveled through Europe like a fat American tourist, eating everything in its path (see "Lousy Bug," page 45). Vineyards were destroyed, wiping out

Europe's wine and brandy industry. The upper classes were stranded with nothing to swirl in their snifters.

Whiskey stepped into the breach. But brandy drinkers were a classy lot. It simply wouldn't *do* to drink out of barrels the way those grotty whiskey drinkers did. So eager-to-please salesmen with now-familiar names like Dewar, Walker, Bell, and Teacher put their product in glass bottles for the first time and pasted on labels, creating brand-name whiskeys. By the time the brandy industry recovered, Scotch had become its permanent replacement in drawing room decanters of the world.

Boom, Bust, Boom

Things were going so well that whiskey became the Internet of the 1890s. It enjoyed a massive boom as banks began investing wildly and unwisely in every hastily built, two-bit distillery. It didn't seem to matter that the entire planet combined wasn't drinking the amount being produced. Distillers were so flush that some started skipping over the middle part, where they were supposed to actually *make* whiskey, and just used the bank loans to build large town houses. Fraud charges were filed, people went to jail, and, like all booms, it went bust.

The only problem was, it didn't stop busting. Barley shortages during World War I sent whiskey prices up. Then the Temperance Movement elected a government that declared—during wartime and with a straight face—that whiskey was a deadlier foe than Germany. It imposed crippling taxes, sending whiskey prices even further up and prompting this 1920 music hall lament:

> *"Twelve an' a tanner a bottle,*
> *That's what it's costing today;*
> *Twelve an' a tanner a bottle—*
> *Man, it taks a' the pleasure away.*

Before you can have a wee drappie
You have tae spend a' that ye've got—
How can a fella be happy,
When happiness costs such a lot."

In 1899, Scotland had 161 distilleries. By 1924, a full 50 percent were bankrupt. But then America's Temperance Movement, led by a very large and very crazy ax-aficionado known as Carry Nation (see "American Prohibition," page 225), decided it would go Britain one better by flat-out banning alcohol.

Prohibition destroyed America's whiskey industry, but the Scottish, well, they'd been smuggling whiskey since before America was born. Quite literally. Go back a few pages and look at those dates again. Exports to "the Bahamas" (wink, wink) went from 25,000 gallons in 1920 to nearly 6 million in 1930.

This was cold comfort to the Irish. In 1921, their country won its independence from Britain but at the cost of a ban on Irish goods throughout the British empire. The Irish whiskey industry was completely decimated.

Irish and American whiskey never fully recovered. And, in their absence, as whiskey has spread around the globe to places like Japan (where it's more popular than sake) and India (which oddly enough has the second most distilleries behind Scotland), Scotch whiskey has become the benchmark against which all other whiskeys are measured.

Scotland's national drink had achieved a status just as mythic as their origins.

BOURBON

Still-Billies

Scotch and bourbon may come from the same whiskey family, but as Scotch got classier, bourbon became its cussin', fightin' cousin. Drinks like Jack Daniel's and Jim Beam have become a permanent sidekick to cowboys, bikers, rock bands, and wannabe bad-asses the world over. And whether they know it or not, these folks are upholding centuries of tradition, because bourbon's been a problem child ever since birth.

Remember all those crusty, antigovernment farmers who made whiskey a rebel drink in Scotland and Ireland? Well, they did it in America, too. In the early 1700s, Scots and Irish began emigrating to America, but they bypassed the populated cities for the first available farmland in the hills to the west. And they brought their stills with them.

Unlike back home, the barley they used to make whiskey didn't grow so well. But rye did, and the German immigrants who settled alongside them had a tradition of distilling rye into schnapps. Together, they came up with rye whiskey.

None of which mattered to anyone outside the farms, because while America was still a British colony, it drank the drink of the seagoing empire—rum (see page 105). But, then, of course, America decided to stop being a colony.

The Shot Heard Round the World

The thing about war that gets frequently lost amidst the rocket's red glare is that it's a darn expensive undertaking. So when the British finally packed their bags, they left behind a country deeply in debt. Desperate to pay America's bills, Alexander Hamilton noticed that when rum shipping halted during the fighting, Americans began buying a lot of this new, homegrown farm liquor. So, in 1791, he introduced the *very first* tax in the United States of America. On whiskey.

Easterners and commercial distilleries shrugged their shoulders and paid up. But out on the frontier (which at that time meant western Pennsylvania), the farmers went ballistic. To be fair, they had a point:

There was no tax when they sold their grain, so why should there be one on whiskey? It was just grain in liquid form. Plus, they were so poor that whiskey was literally their form of currency. But most of all, and more to the point, they were a bunch of ornery, backwoods hicks who liked to get drunk.

> "THREE DRINKS OF MOUNTAIN DEW CAUSE ON AVERAGE ONE FIGHT."—*THE AMERICAN JOURNAL OF SOCIOLOGY*, JULY 1901

They voiced their objections in a variety of ways. Mail was intercepted and warrants torn up. Tax collectors were tarred and feathered. The movement even developed its own mythological figure, Tom the Tinker, a sort of B-grade Robin Hood whose name was invoked every time someone shot up the stills of the commercial distilleries that paid their taxes. After three years of this, it began creating real problems for the country.

On a practical level, it was a test of the nation's all-important ability to collect a tax, any tax. Ideologically, the Founding Fathers feared this rebellion would inspire secession movements (western Pennsylvania had already picked its snappy new name, Westsylvania). And there were fears (only partly true) that Britain was stoking this rebellion in the hopes of splintering America into weak, easily conquerable breakaway republics. So, ideologically, there was a lot at stake. But in reality, and again, more to the point, the Whiskey Rebellion was comprised of a bunch of ornery, backwoods hicks who liked to get drunk.

The situation reached its boiling point in July of 1794, when a local militia torched the house of John Neville, a tax collector who was a boyhood friend of Washington's and a general in the Revolutionary War.

The leaders of the rebellion then gathered six thousand men on the outskirts of Pittsburgh with the intention of taking the town and declaring all-out war. The Pittsburghians, however, devised a clever ploy.

They informed the militia that, by sheer coincidence, they too were big fans of free whiskey, and to prove it, they handed the militia all the free whiskey it wanted. Well, this was the sort of hospitality a rebellion could really get behind. A party broke out and the militia forgot all about invading Pittsburgh.

> "WHISKEY'LL MAKE A NEW MAN OUT OF YOU. BUT THEN HE HAS TO HAVE A DRINK."
> —WILD WEST PROVERB

But the good times ended with the sobering news that a very pissed-off George Washington had mobilized an army of almost thirteen thousand men (bigger than the one that had fought the Revolution), and was personally marching toward Pennsylvania.

The rebellion evaporated, and by the time Washington's army arrived in the region, there was no one to fight. The tax survived, and despite many alterations, it's still in existence today, making it the oldest tax in United States history.

As for the rebels, some went home and some moved west over the Appalachians and into Kentucky, where they thought the tax collectors couldn't reach them. They were wrong, but there in Kentucky they discovered three things that made up for it.

Whiskey River

Limestone water, corn, and charred oak barrels. The three pillars of bourbon.

This especially pure water sprang up from the blue hills of Kentucky. And planting corn was a bit of advice the settlers took from the Indians before they began handing out the smallpox blankets. Virtually unheard-of in Europe, corn grew fantastically in North America, and it distilled well, too.

As for barrels, no one quite knows who thought of charring them first, but legend has it that a Kentucky preacher/distiller named Elijah Craig had a fire in his small distillery that badly burned his barrels. Being a thrifty Scotsman, he refused to throw them away, and filled them with the same clear corn whiskey everyone was making at the time. The burned wood gave color and flavor to the whiskey and Elijah's neighbors copied him.

As for the name, it's a bit ironic, but bourbon—that take-no-shit-from-the-law kind of liquor—is actually named after the French royal family. In gratitude for France's help during the Revolution, the United States carved a huge whack off Kentucky in 1785 and named it after the House of Bourbon. (As a further irony, the American Revolution inspired France's own revolution, which resulted in many Bourbon beheadings.)

Heavy trade sprang up as Bourbon County loaded its whiskey and hemp (no foolin') onto boats and shipped them downriver to New Orleans. And between the wood, water, corn, and the distilling talents of those displaced Whiskey Rebels, folks in the Big Easy immediately noticed that out of all the frontier settlements making whiskey, the barrels marked "Old Bourbon" were the best. People started asking for it by name. Distillers from other counties quickly utilized a marketing technique known as "lying," and labeled their barrels "Old Bourbon" as well. Soon enough, "bourbon" became the general term for any whiskey distilled from corn.

It also became big business. By the 1830s, Americans were drinking an average of six gallons of bourbon a year (that's twenty-four times more than today). By 1850, Pennsylvania alone had three thousand registered stills. Small backwoods distillers turned into large commercial distilleries, and by 1862, taxes on whiskey accounted for a quarter of the government's total revenue. Bourbon and the United States were expanding hand in hand, and by the same means. They hopped on a railroad car and rode off into the West.

Go West, My Son

If one of the first signs of a civilization is an economy, then you can tell a lot about a culture by what it spends its money on. And in Dodge City, the infamous epitome of a Wild West town, the first business establishment was a tent that sold whiskey.

The United States needed whiskey as badly as a rummy with the shakes. As settlers pushed farther and farther west, Washington's grip on them became weaker and weaker. Taxes on liquor were the only way to get money from its far-flung citizens. Many westerners on the losing side of the Civil War would be damned if they gave a nickel to the government, but they practically handed their wallets to the bartenders. By 1876, with a population of only twelve hundred, Dodge managed to support nineteen whiskey saloons (beer didn't arrive until 1879). And while movies have portrayed the Wild West as a place of rough men drinking rough whiskey roughly, you don't know the half of it.

What they were drinking may have left Kentucky as bourbon, but by the time it reached a cowboy's lips, it had been stepped on so many times by middlemen that a shot of "bourbon" was more likely to be industrial alcohol flavored with tobacco, pepper, prune juice, or soap. Little wonder that western whiskey earned itself nicknames like coffin varnish, tanglefoot, Taos lightning, and tarantula juice.

But bourbon makers didn't take this lying down. These weren't scruffy farmers anymore, they were guys who had the southern gentlemen thing down to an art. They were rich, powerful, prone to using military titles, and one thing you did *not* do was mess with their bourbon.

One such specimen was Colonel Taylor, the creator of Old Taylor bourbon, who turned his southern-fried charm on Congress to convince them that "the ancient bourbon flavor has departed and the stomach groans under the dominion of the new ruler." He succeeded, and in 1897, Congress passed the Bottled-in-Bond Act. This governmental guarantee of whiskey's quality was the *first* federal consumer protection ever created in the United States. (The House of Representatives seems to have a particular fondness—bourbon is now the official drink of the United States Congress.)

> "I'M A CHRISTIAN, BUT THAT DOESN'T MEAN I'M A LONG-FACED SQUARE. I LIKE A LITTLE BOURBON."—PRESIDENT JIMMY CARTER'S MOTHER

So with its aura as the all-American liquor, thousands of distilleries throughout the nation, and its quality assured by the U.S. government, bourbon stepped confidently into the twentieth century. Where it ran straight into a brick wall. Prohibition.

The End of the Line

In the final tally, American Prohibition dealt its harshest blow to American whiskey.

Distilleries closed, of course, but that was true for every liquor. No, the thing that really hurt bourbon was a little bit of Canadian/Scottish schadenfreude. The two countries gleefully took advantage of bourbon's misfortune by flooding the speakeasies with their own blended whiskeys. People enjoyed this lighter style and became so accustomed to it that by the time Prohibition was repealed thirteen years later, bourbon's and rye's heavy flavors were totally out of fashion.

American whiskey never fully recovered. By the early 1990s, Kentucky only had ten distilleries. Tennessee just two. And while bourbon has begun making a comeback by catering to the high-end, small-batch market that Scotch created, it's a far cry from its glory days as the liquor that helped forge a new nation.

USELESS INFO

The Snakebite Cure with Bite

In the nineteenth century, the recommended cure for a snakebite was two *pints* of 100-proof bourbon. If the bite didn't kill you, the cure sure would.

Whiskey Killer

The deadliest cat ever recorded was "Towser," the house tabby for the Glenturret Distillery. With the barrel-aging rooms as his killing fields (and some obviously bored distillers keeping score), he managed to dispatch 28,899 mice in his lifetime.

Drink Money

The pot stills used by Macallan are the smallest in Scotland and are so distinctive, they're featured on the back of the Scottish ten-pound note.

Trouser Troubles

Nineteenth-century Irish police received a "britches allowance," extra money to pay for damage incurred to their trousers while chasing moonshiners through hills and undergrowth.

Barfly Advice

Whether true or not, barfly legend has long maintained that whiskey, if used as the primary source of inebriation over a period of several years, has an adverse effect upon a man's sexual abilities. This process is alternately known as "whiskey dick," or "brewer's droop."

An Honorable Wager

Local barbershop, 1924: While getting a haircut, James Beauregard Beam (aka Jim Beam) was lamenting Prohibition's effect on the bourbon industry. Why, it was so bad, he declared, he had half a mind to sell the whole dern Beam Distillery to the first man who offered him a measly ten grand. Now, in a stroke of bad luck, the man in the barber chair next to him was a notorious gambler named Will Styles.

Styles took up this semifacetious offer, and Beam, being a southern gentleman, honored his word. Legal records show that Styles had ownership of the Jim Beam distillery for twelve months, during which he sold all the warehoused whiskey over the Canadian border for $400,000. Once it was emptied, he handed the distillery back, leaving Mr. Beam poorer, but with a word that was good as gold.

Stock Cars, Stocked Bars

Most incidents involving whiskey, car chases, and cops end badly for all concerned. But, in America, it ended up as the number-one spectator sport in the country— NASCAR.

In the American South during Prohibition, back-woods moonshiners had to stay one step ahead of the law while running their whiskey into town. And the fastest way to do that was with the new fangled automobile.

Moonshine runners began leading police on high-speed chases through curvy mountain roads in the middle of the night. It required the best drivers with the most souped-up cars available, because losing meant a deadly crash or heavy jailtime. To hone their skills, drivers began practicing on Sunday afternoons in friendly competitions. Crowds gathered, and NASCAR was born.

Tight Little Island

In 1941, the Nazi blitz was destroying London's warehouses. To save their whiskey, distributors loaded their reserves onto ships bound for Jamaica. One ship never made it.

On February 5, 1941, the SS *Politician* ran aground near the Scottish fishing island of Eriskay (pop. 200). After being rescued by the locals, the crew let slip the contents of their cargo: 28,000 cases of grade-A Scottish whiskey.

Eriskay was a "dry" island at the time, and with 264,000 bottles of Scotch lying just off the coast, all hell broke loose. Fishing stopped entirely as boats raided the wreckage of *Polly*, as the ship became affectionately known.

British tax officials, insurance agents, and salvage crews descended on the island to stake their claim to *Polly*. And since Eriskay is only 3 miles long by 1.5 miles wide, locals struggled to find room to hide a quarter-million bottles: under haystacks, in holes dug in the ground, inside walls and ceilings of houses, even under beds rented out to the visiting officials.

The story inspired a classic (though slightly dated) British film, *Whisky Galore!*

　　ALCOHOLICA ESOTERICA

The Whiskey "e"

In Ireland and America, it's spelled "whiskey." In Britain and Canada, it's "whisky." There's no rhyme or reason why they started spelling it differently, they just did. So it's pretty uninteresting. Let's move on.

The Whiskey Wheel

This is the flavor chart developed by whiskeyologists that rates it in the following categories: clean, fruity, green/grassy, green/oily, meaty, metallic, musty, nutty, peaty, perfumed, sour, spicy, sulfury, sweet, vegetable, and waxy.

Neat or No?

Regarding the great debate of whether to mix ice and/or water with your whiskey, no one agrees. Proponents of the Drink-It-Like-a-Man school quote the Scottish proverb: "Never drink whiskey with water, and never drink water without whiskey."

However, most experts add a little water to bring out the flavor and aroma better. As to how much to add, well, that's even more personal, or as the Irish saying goes, "Never steal a man's wife, and never water another man's whiskey."

Legs

Swirl your whiskey for a moment, then stop. The viscous film on the side of the glass will begin to slide down in drops called the "legs." The faster the legs run, the lighter the whiskey.

Older Isn't Always Better

Older whiskey may cost more, but that doesn't necessarily make it better. Whiskey gets most of its color and flavor from the barrel, so it all depends on the barrels they're aged in. For instance, bourbon is aged in charred barrels, so anything past ten or twelve years tends to taste like . . . well . . . charred barrels, really.

Scotch, on the other hand, is aged in barrels previously used for bourbon, sherry, or port. Used barrels take longer for the flavor to come out. But even then, only the best scotches benefit from twenty-five years of aging. Best to read up on it before dropping a couple hundred bucks.

Blend versus Single-Malt

A blend can contain as many as forty whiskeys, including whiskey made from corn, oats, and rye. This gives blends a lighter flavor and texture than most single malts, which are 100 percent barley and come from only one distillery.

Scottish Whiskey

Scotch is malt whiskey, meaning its made from barley, which is dried using burning peat, hence the smoky flavor. By law, Scotch has to be aged a minimum of three years *in Scotland*. Scotch is divided into four basic geographical/flavor groups:

Lowlands (southern Scotland): Soft, grassy, subtle.
Highlands (northern Scotland): Contains many
    distilleries, so covers a broad range of styles.
    Generally aromatic, medium-bodied.
Speyside: Light, sweet, fruity.
The Islands: Tends to be the strongest, very smoky
    and peaty, sea-air salty.

Irish Whiskey

A blend of barley, corn, and rye. Dried with kilns, not peat, hence none of Scotch's smokiness. Distilled three times as opposed to Scotch's two, giving it a full-bodied, smooth, fruitier flavor.

American Whiskey

Bourbon: By law, must be at least 51 percent corn and aged for a minimum of two years in newly charred oak barrels. No blending is permitted. Corn whiskey tends to be fuller-bodied and sweeter than malt whiskey.

Tennessee whiskey: The same as bourbon except distilled in Tennessee—natch—and filtered through sugar-maple charcoal, which makes it smoother and mellower.

Sour mash: A process where the yeast mixture from a previous batch is used to start a new fermentation going. In the old days, this created consistency in taste between different batches. But in modern times, fermentation is so scientific it makes no difference. Distillers just print "sour mash" on bottles now because it sounds cooler.

Canadian Whiskey

Halfway between bourbon and Scotch. Like bourbon, it's made primarily from corn. But like Scotch, it's frequently aged in used barrels. Almost all Canadian whiskeys are blends and tend to be light-bodied, slightly pale, and mellow.

Fifteen Great Country Drinking Songs

Beer, bars, and broken hearts—country singers are the poet laureates of drinking. And while there are thousands of country songs dealing with the combustible mixture of alcohol and heartache, here are some of the best song titles to come out of Nashville.

"What Made Milwaukee Famous (Has Made a Loser Out of Me)"

"She's Acting Single, and I'm Drinking Doubles"

"Rednecks, White Socks and Pabst Blue Ribbon Beer"

"Don't Come Home a-Drinkin' with Lovin' on Your Mind"

"Get Off the Table, Mabel (the Two Dollars Is for the Beer)"

"I'm Drinkin' Christmas Dinner (All Alone This Year)"

"Why Don't We Get Drunk and Screw?"

"I'm Going to Hire a Wino to Decorate Our Home"

"I Want a Beer as Cold as My Ex-Wife's Heart"

"You Ain't Much Fun Since I Quit Drinkin'"

"It Only Takes One Bar (To Make a Prison)"

On the Perils of Alcohol and Ugly Women

"I Haven't Gone to Bed with Any Ugly Women But I've Sure Woke Up with a Few"

"Got In at 2 with a 10, And Woke Up at 10 with a 2"

"Don't All the Girls Get Prettier at Closing Time"

"She's Looking Better After Every Beer"

RUM

HOW A DARK CHAPTER IN HUMAN HISTORY LEARNED TO LIGHTEN UP AND GO ON VACATION

Sweet Beginnings

"Texas tea! White gold! Sugar!" —HOMER SIMPSON

Pirates, slaves, Cubans, and doughboys—the history of rum is rife with the sort of characters that make for ripping adventure novels. Like most tales of adventure, it began as a hunt for treasure. In this case, the treasure was sugar and the action took a while to get going. 8,500 years, in fact.

That's how long it took for sugarcane to migrate from its prehistoric origins in Papua New Guinea to the Caribbean. Along the way, "the reed which gives honey without the help of bees" encountered Chinese traders who spread it to Asia and India, Alexander the Great who spread it into the Middle East, and then Moorish invaders who brought it to the shores of southern Europe.

The final leg of the relay was completed by

Christopher Columbus himself, who traveled to the New World in search of gold, not knowing that he already had something just as valuable onboard. In 1493, Columbus planted the Caribbean's first sugarcane on the island of Haiti. It grew like wildfire, a white gold mine waiting for someone to feed Europe's insatiable sweet tooth.

But the Spaniards weren't done beating a dead horse yet and virtually ignored sugarcane as they searched for yellow gold. By the time they caught on to their mistake, the Portuguese, English, French, and Dutch were all piling into the Caribbean, transforming it into one giant sugar factory.

The only real downside to producing sugar was its inefficiency. Boiling cane juice creates granular sugar and a sludgy black residue we now know as molasses. Back then, molasses was just a waste product, but they were loath to throw away anything that sweet. So the British tried fermenting and distilling it and on the island of Barbados the first rum was produced.

Sailor's Delight

It wasn't called rum, though. That came later, in 1672, probably descending from "rumbullion," a British slang term for "an uproar, a great tumult." This seems like a pretty accurate description because before it was rum, it was mainly known as Kill-Devil.

It was described in 1650 as "a hott, hellish and terrible liquor," and was only deemed fit for the slaves, who used it to cure illnesses and conjure up spirits (see "Ogoun," page 191). But despite its terrible flavor, this new liquor began to prove very useful, not just internally, but politically as well.

As the European countries jockeyed for power in the islands, they paid pirates to harass the trading ships and plantations of their rivals. In 1655, for instance, the English seized Jamaica from Spain with the help of Captain Henry Morgan (of spiced rum fame), a much-feared buccaneer who used his payment to buy a plantation, grow rich, and get knighted as Sir Henry Morgan, the deputy governor of Jamaica.

To prevent this, plantation owners needed protection, and they quickly discovered that distilling rum ensured a steady flow of British naval vessels into their ports. And where the British navy dropped anchor, pirates steered clear.

> "Fifteen men on a dead man's chest
> Yo ho ho and a bottle of rum
> Drink and the devil have done for the rest
> Yo ho ho and a bottle of rum."
>
> —Robert Louis Stevenson, *Treasure Island*

Sailors—pirates and navy men alike—had their own reasons for liking Kill-Devil. Namely, they were sick of beer. But wait, that isn't as unforgivable as it sounds. Beer was a sailor's only relief from the wretched conditions onboard, but during long journeys it turned brackish and foul as it cooked in the sweltering holds of ships passing through tropical waters.

Rum was much more durable, and it proved so popular that, in 1740, the British Royal Navy instituted something that pirates had been doing for decades, issuing a daily ration of a half-pint of 160-proof rum (for more on the British navy's quasi-sexual relationship with rum, see "British Royal Navy," page 204).

The British Royal Navy was the most powerful military force in the world by then. And rum was now its official beverage of choice.

British traders began shuttling this new liquor between the Old World and the New. But it really wasn't catching on in the Old World. There's a large gulf between the drinking abilities of seventeenth-century sailors and that of mere mortals, and this early rum was liquid dynamite, a harsh, clear fluid bottled directly from the still. In 1698, England only imported 207 gallons.

But as the Navy and trading ships drank more and more, distillers had to increase production. They began storing their excess rum in barrels, where it soaked up the color and flavor of the wood and lost its harsh edge. Kill-Devil became "comfortable water." And the New World wasn't as shy as the Old; America took to this water like a fish.

Actually, the American colonies took to *any* alcohol like a fish. It was a hard-living, hard-drinking sort of place. Every town was required by law to have a tavern, which also doubled as the town hall, jailhouse, and hospital when necessary. Alcohol was consumed morning, noon, and night—beer and cider mostly, since wine and brandy had to be imported at great cost all the way from Europe.

But rum . . . rum came from America's next-door neighbor. So it was cheap and it was strong. And when British ships sailed into port with the first barrels, Americans treated it like manna from the heavens.

"IF THE ANCIENTS DRANK WINE AS OUR PEOPLE DRINK RUM AND CIDER, IT'S NO WONDER WE HEAR OF SO MANY POSSESSED WITH DEVILS." —PRESIDENT JOHN ADAMS

Rum became the American colonies' number-one commercial industry and its number-one exported good. Unfortunately, America liked rum a little too much, because it was willing to do some pretty awful things to get it.

Middle Passage

The plantations had a problem: to generate enough sugar for one thousand gallons of rum required a workforce of approximately three hundred people. By 1770, England alone, having discovered the joys of rum punch, was importing 2 million gallons of rum. Someone needed to do all the work.

The Europeans certainly weren't going to. Not in that ghastly heat. And the native Indians on the islands were too busy dying from diseases the Europeans brought with them. The solution was slavery; the Triangular Trade was born.

First, plantations would export molasses to England, France, and America for distilling. Then, ships would travel to the west coast of Africa and use rum to purchase slaves from local African kings who'd developed a jones for the drink. The slaves were then shipped to the Caribbean via the brutal Middle Passage. The ones who survived were sent out into the cane fields, where they encountered tropical heat, disease, poisonous snakes, and sometimes the misswung machetes of other workers. The plantations had a voracious appetite.

In the eighteenth century alone, the sugar colonies purchased over 4 million slaves.

The Triangular Trade was such good business that shipping cities like Liverpool, Bordeaux, and even hoity-toity Newport, Rhode Island, were built on its profits. So woe betide anyone who tried to mess with America's rum trade. Woe betide Britain.

Revolution, Devolution

The British ran their empire like a mob racket, with one colony buying goods from another at inflated prices and the king pocketing the profit. All America wanted was a drink, and the cheaper, the better. So when it started buying inexpensive rum from the French and Spanish islands, Parliament decided to break some kneecaps. It passed the Molasses Act in 1733, imposing heavy fines on imports from non-British islands.

But as the empire was starting to find out, it was awfully hard to break kneecaps from across an ocean. The act was evaded and outright ignored. Forty years before the Boston Tea Party, most historians credit America's rebellion against the Molasses Act as its first major act of civil disobedience.

> "I KNOW NOT WHY WE SHOULD BLUSH TO CONFESS THAT MOLASSES WAS AN ESSENTIAL INGREDIENT IN AMERICAN INDEPENDENCE."
> —PRESIDENT JOHN ADAMS

Ironically, even though America's love of rum helped kick off the Revolutionary War, it was the Revolutionary War that killed America's love of rum. It disrupted ocean trade, forcing America to turn away from the sea as its source of liquor and look to the land. And American soil grew barley, corn, and rye, not sugarcane. America became a whiskey nation.

To make matters worse, the Napoleonic Wars in the early 1800s halted *Europe's* shipping trade, too. Caribbean sugar supplies dried up; French pastries were in danger of going unsweetened. Acting swiftly, Napoleon ordered scientists to harness the power of the beet for its sugar-producing abilities. Crisis averted, but sugarcane was no longer necessary. The Caribbean and rum fell on hard times.

Desperate for money, island distillers began selling cut-rate rum of questionable quality to America, earning it a reputation as a skid-row drink. In the presidential election of 1900, an early version of the Republican attack machine came up with this slogan:

"McKinley drinks soda water,
Bryan drinks rum,
McKinley is a gentleman,
Bryan is a bum."

Rum, which had comforted the colonies and inspired a revolution, had now become America's prodigal son, cast out and clucked over. It had become Demon Rum, and it was public enemy number one to the Prohibition League that was gaining momentum in the late 1800s. But while they were declaring war on rum, rum was developing some new weapons of its own down in Cuba.

Cuba Libre!

In 1829, a Spanish wine merchant named Don Facundo Bacardi moved to Cuba. He took a liking to the indigenous drink and began experimenting with its distillation in his backyard. When he finally got the recipe right, he bought a small distillery in 1862 and introduced a whole new style to the world—light rum.

While this doesn't seem huge, it was. Light rum was smoother and mellower than the harsh dark rums, making it the perfect alcohol for mixed drinks. Not only did this inspire other distillers to put their Kill-Devil days behind them and create higher-quality rum, it inspired two Americans who came to Cuba with Teddy Roosevelt and his Rough Riders in 1898. One (an engineer) created the daiquiri, and another (a soldier) created the Cuba Libre, otherwise known as a rum-and-Coke.

So when Prohibition finally arrived in 1920, rum was ready to impress. Americans flocked to Havana (the nearest legal watering hole), where the bartenders were waiting with a daiquiri in one hand and a

Cuba Libre in the other. These two new drinks helped boost rum's reputation, but only among Americans who could afford to travel to another country for a nightcap. Most poor slobs had to make do with whatever bootleggers gave them, and gin and whiskey were the preferred contraband.

No, to get back into the hearts, minds, and livers of America again, rum needed something big, something really earth-shattering to help. Like a world war.

The Fruits of War

If the Revolutionary War killed rum, World War II brought it back to life. Fourteen separate military bases were built throughout the Caribbean islands. And while these members of the greatest generation surely served their country to their utmost, they had a slightly more laid-back time of it than, say, the ones on Omaha Beach, and were able to develop an appreciation for the local rums.

Meanwhile, back on the mainland, Europe's liquor exports had stopped and America diverted all its domestic alcohol production toward the war effort. America was left bone-dry, and that's just no way to go through a war. The Caribbean suddenly found itself living next to a very thirsty customer. So when the war was over (because we won), many soldiers returned to discover a nation awash in their favorite new drink.

"THE GREAT UTILITY OF RUM HAS GIVEN IT THE MEDICAL NAME OF AN ANTIFOGMATIC. THE QUANTITY TAKEN EVERY MORNING IS IN EXACT PROPORTION TO THE THICKNESS OF THE FOG."
—ANONYMOUS IN *MASSACHUSETTS SPY* NEWSPAPER, 1789

Postwar prosperity cemented rum's popularity (try saying *that* five times fast). The tiki-lounge craze canonized a host of new rum drinks and the rise of air-conditioning made the Caribbean an easy and popular tourist destination. And whether they were aware of it or not, by lying on those white-sand beaches and sipping daiquiris, Americans were getting back to their roots, to the drink that fueled their forefathers and the foundation of their country.

Rum and America, at last, were happily reunited.

USELESS INFO

Family Planning

- In nineteenth-century England, men would occasionally auction off their wives in exchange for rum.

- In the Caribbean, rum is sprinkled on a newborn baby's forehead for luck.

Slave Punch Singsong

The original recipe for Planter's Punch was based on a work song chanted by slaves in the cane fields: "One of sour [lime], two of sweet [sugar], three of strong [rum], and four of weak [ice]."

Aussie Hospital

The first hospital built in Australia was Rum Hospital (1816). It was so named because the builders were paid with the closest thing Australia had to a winning lottery ticket—a license to import rum to the thirsty Australians.

Rum City

Belize City is built on bottles of rum. Actually, it's built on reclaimed swampland, but when workers were chopping trees into mulch to form usable ground, they would drink rum—a *lot* of rum—and toss the empty bottles alongside the mulch. In 1909, a British officer describing Belize City noted, "You may dig down a well 50 to 100 feet, and you will still find mahogany chips and rum bottles!"

The Bacardi Bat

Why does a bat appear on every bottle of Bacardi rum? The company's official story is that Don Facundo founded Bacardi by purchasing a small distillery that had a family of fruit bats living in the rafters. Most people were illiterate at the time so Facundo's wife suggested using the bats, a Cuban symbol of good luck, as a logo on the bottle.

A less PR-friendly version of the story I've heard from a member of the Bacardi family is that when Facundo was first experimenting with rum in a shack in his backyard, he left a batch to sit for several days. Upon returning, he discovered that a bat had flown into the open vat of rum. It tumbled to the ground in front of him, flopped around in a drunken stupor for several minutes, and then died. The bat was proof that Bacardi made potent stuff and it went on the label.

Party Animals

An outpost of the Indian army in the jungle region of Bagdógra has been under attack ever since a local herd of elephants raided the base in search of food and found the soldiers' entire winter ration of rum. Since then, the pachyderms have regularly raided the base for a drink, smashing down all defenses put up by the army, including electrified fences and firewalls.

According to the *Daily Telegraph*, "An officer recently posted there explained that the elephants broke the rum bottles by cleverly curling their trunks around the bottom. Then they empty the contents down their throats. They soon got drunk, he said, and swayed around. They enjoy themselves and then return to the jungle."

> "BUNDABERG RUM, OVERPROOF RUM, WILL TAN YOUR INSIDES AND GROW HAIR ON YOUR BUM."—BILL SCOTT, AUSTRALIAN POET

USEFUL INFO

Island Hopping

Rum is *the* drink of the Caribbean, and each island has developed its own distinct style. Puerto Rico, Barbados, and the Virgin Islands, for instance, tend toward light rum, while former French colonies like Haiti and Martinique make dark, aromatic rums that pattern themselves after French brandy.

The Rum Family

There are two basic styles of rum:

- **Light/white:** Distilled and filtered like vodka, with an eye toward removing all impurities, including much of the flavor. Usually aged for only a few months. This is the ideal rum for mixed drinks and is best served cold. If white rum is barrel-aged for several years, it becomes the medium-bodied "golden rum."

- **Dark/black:** Distilled like cognac and whiskey for maximum flavor and depth. The dark color is produced by adding caramel. Barrel-aged a minimum of three to five years. Dark, sipping rums are technically supposed to be drunk neat, at room temperature, but adding a little water or allowing an ice cube to melt in it helps release some of the flavors and aromas.

Age without Vintage

Unlike grapes, sugarcane's flavor doesn't change according to soil and climate. Therefore, rum's flavor is achieved through distilling and blending, so there are no vintages. However, some *añejo* ("aged") sipping rums (usually dark) will carry an age date (ten-year, twenty-year, etc.). This means that the *youngest* rum blended into that bottle was ten years old, the others can be much older.

"WHAT'S THE USE OF THUNDER? . . . WE DON'T WANT THUNDER; WE WANT RUM; GIVE US A GLASS OF RUM!"

—HERMAN MELVILLE, *MOBY-DICK*

GIN

"I'm tired of gin,
I'm tired of sin,
And after last night,
Oh boy, am I tired."
 —ANONYMOUS

Today, it's the genteel drink, the tipple of the top-hat set.

But the story of gin is the same as *Pygmalion*, or *Pretty Woman*, for the more Julia Roberts–inclined. Because like a high-price hooker done good, if you looked at gin today, you'd never realize how sordid its history really was . . .

The Black Plague Berry

Europe, fourteenth century: The Black Plague claimed 25 million lives. The Grim Reaper stalked the land, and the only way to stop him was to give him a case of the runs. Or something like that. For whatever reason, the juniper berry (a mild diuretic) was considered a miracle drug, able to repel the plague and also, clear up your gout.

People wore masks filled with juniper berries and used it as flavoring in their drink. So when the Dutch began making brandy in the fourteenth century (see "Brandy, page 134), juniper was a familiar additive to wine. Plus, they discovered that it helped mask any flaws in a bad batch. Juniper-infusion became a regular practice for the Dutch, but grapes aren't readily available in the Netherlands, so they also distilled it into alcohol made from grain.

By the fifteenth century, every town in the Netherlands had a juniper liquor or, as they called it, "genever." Pretty soon, they were exporting this drink as a health tonic all over Europe, including into England, where it became a curiosity drink for the idle rich.

But the history of gin changed radically once England's commoners got their hands on it, and it literally almost destroyed England.

How to Get a Country Drunk without Really Trying

When the Thirty Years' War ended in 1648, English soldiers and sailors left the battlefields of the Netherlands with a taste for what they called "dutch courage." But for several decades, gin remained the dockside drink of sailors, until 1689, when a new king of England was crowned—William of Orange. A Dutchman.

After that, events conspired very quickly:

1. Gin was now the drink of the king's court. It was hip.

2. In 1690, some powerful landowners pushed the 1690 Distilling Act through Parliament. Before then, commoners only drank beer and cider because England had no distilling industry of its own. The wealthy could import French brandy, but that was the only hard alcohol available.

The Distilling Act encouraged the production of English spirits. Not coincidentally, this gave the landowners a lucrative new market for their grain (gin is three-quarters corn and one-quarter barley).

3. To favor his homeland and punish the French, William of Orange banned the importation of French brandy. Gin was now cheaper than brandy.

4. In 1694, beer was heavily taxed. Gin was now the cheapest drink in England.

5. New laws allowed every Tom, Dick, and Nigel to home-brew liquor. Home brewers quickly realized that gin was ideal. It didn't require any barrel aging. Plus, to save money on alcohol, they could cut it with things like turpentine and sulfuric acid and cover their tracks with the heavy juniper flavor.

    In fact, "gin" was originally a sarcastic term used by the rich to distinguish the commoner's rotgut (which tended to be a liver-lashing 160 proof) from their top-shelf imported Dutch "genever."

6. Finally, a minor bylaw in the 1720 Mutiny Act excused any distiller from having soldiers billeted with him. In other words, shopkeepers were given the choice: make liquor or have a soldier staying in your home, eating your food and hitting on your daughter. . . . They made gin.

"THE SHORTEST WAY OUT OF MANCHESTER IS NOTORIOUSLY A BOTTLE OF GORDON'S GIN." —WILLIAM BOLITHO

And London went, for all intents and purposes, completely bat-shit.

Ladies' Delight, Mother's Ruin

Historians regularly compare London's eighteenth-century gin craze with America's 1980s crack epidemic. Both were born in the ghetto. London was still basically a medieval town—the poor lived in wretched, filthy conditions, always one step away from debtor's prison. Few could resist the popular advertisement of "strong water" shops:

> *"Drunk for a penny, dead drunk for two pence, and straw for nothing."*

The straw was important because, day and night, London was falling-down drunk. The English were old hands at drinking beer, but high-proof gin was a new experience for them, and they didn't handle it so well. A government report concluded that gin left people "no time to recollect or think, whether he has had enough or not. The smallness of the quantity deceives him, so that his Reason is gone before he is aware."

> "GIN! GIN! A DROP OF GIN!
> WHAT MAGNIFIED MONSTERS CIRCLE
> THEREIN!"
>
> —THOMAS HOOD

They were drinking more than small quantities. In 1689, all of England produced about half a million gallons of gin. By 1733, London alone produced and consumed about 6 million gallons. In 1750, London consumed 11 million gallons. And here's the real kicker—at that point, London had a population of just over 600,000 people.

And now for the double kicker: that was only *official* numbers. Gin was being made and sold privately in one out of three homes in parts of the city, or in carts on the street, or if you couldn't afford a full bottle, you could buy a gin-soaked rag to suck on.

This open distribution made all the difference. Previously, alcohol like beer had been served in pubs, the province of men. But with gin selling out in the open, women began to drink. Heavily. Gin was known as "Ladies' Delight" and eventually, "Mother's Ruin."

Women prostituted themselves to buy gin. Gin was used to induce back-alley abortions. Midwives fed gin to newborn babies to quiet them. Between 1730 and 1749, 75 percent of all children christened in London were buried before the age of five. The death rate exceeded the birth rate. Gin was literally killing London.

What with all the misery and wretchedness and fear of the poor spreading plagues (see "Spontaneous Human Combustion," page 203), it was really putting the wealthy off their "genever." Parliament decided to do something about it.

> "NOTHING IS MORE PLEASURABLE THAN TO SIT IN THE SHADE, SIP GIN AND CONTEMPLATE OTHER PEOPLE'S ADULTERIES."
>
> —JOHN SKOW

They didn't bother being real subtle about whom they were targeting. Declaring they would make gin "come so dear to the consumer that the poor will not be able to launch into excessive use of them," they tried taxing gin. Riots ensued; gin endured. They tried banning gin. Riots ensued; black markets rose up (women sold bottles under their skirts); gin endured.

It seemed as if nothing short of a natural disaster could stop gin. Which is exactly what happened. A bad drought hit English crops from 1757 to 1760, making gin so scarce and expensive that bootleggers dried up. Gin fever cooled . . . somewhat.

Been Down So Long, It Looks Like Up from Here

"The ardent spirit that rose from the gutter to become the respectable companion of civilized man."
—LORD KINROSS

By the early 1800s, the rabble were still wretched drunks (see "Gin Palaces," page 121), but the worst excesses were over.

With the black market gone and prices increasing, large-scale gin distillers (Gordon, Beefeater, Tanqueray) went into business. And while the snobbishness of London's high society may make for dull art films, it improved the quality of gin. The gin barons' wealth and place on the social circuit rested squarely on the quality of their product. Gin became drier, clearer, more pure. And as quality improved, gin's reputation improved.

So by the time London started exporting gin in 1850, it had a reputation as a darn good drink. And with the British empire sprawled across the globe, gin had plenty of thirsty colonial officers with walrus mustaches and white hats to service.

British soldiers have been historically adept at sneaking alcohol into their daily regimens (see "British Royal Navy," page 204). In India, they were required to drink a daily dose of tonic water with quinine to combat malaria. Gin, they discovered, nullified the bitter tonic taste. Plus, it proved the perfect companion for those grueling three-day cricket matches. The gin and tonic paraded home to England with the aura of empire upon it.

Suddenly, it was okay for Victorian ladies to serve gin during high tea, although they referred to it primly as "white wine."

Puttin' on the Ritz

By now, gin was a pretty classy dame, but it went through finishing school during the American Prohibition. Just like London's gin craze, Prohibition gave rise to black markets and rotgut bathtub gin. In 1924, four thousand Americans died from bad alcohol.

That didn't stop people from drinking. It just gave them incentive to search for high-quality stuff. Gin, specifically, because it proved to be the perfect mixer for the newly invented drink known as the "cocktail" that became the semiofficial stimulant of Prohibition (see "Cocktails," page 151). And London gin was the best.

The price of a bottle smuggled across the Atlantic was exorbitant, but the alternative was possible blindness or death. If you could afford it, you drank it. Only the rich could afford it, only the rich drank it. So gin stepped out of Prohibition like a newly arrived debutante.

It was "Mother's Ruin" no more. It was Gin, the genteel drink, the tipple of the top-hat set.

USELESS INFO

Ripped

Rip Van Winkle, in the original Washington Irving story, is "naturally a thirsty soul," and he falls into his twenty-year sleep after drinking an entire flagon of something that "had much of the flavour of excellent Hollands." In other words, gin.

An American First

The first distillery in the United States was built on Staten Island in 1640 by the Dutch to produce gin, their home country's hip new drink.

Getting Your Bearings

Next time you look at a compass, you can think of gin. Many nineteenth-century English explorers were funded by gin barons seeking respectability. And one such expedition in the early 1830s established the true position of the North Magnetic Pole.

Gin Palaces

To combat London's gin craze, beer drinking was officially encouraged. Breweries were allowed to loan money to pub owners to spruce up their pubs and draw in customers. Gin shops had to compete, so they did it Las Vegas–style, glossing over gin's grimy reputation with a lot of glitter. They transformed themselves into "gin palaces," some of which still exist in London.

These were gaudy, vaulting pubs with huge mirrors and ornate wood carvings intended to provide some escapism for the miserable lower classes. Charles Dickens noted that gin palaces were "invariably numerous and splendid in precise proportion to the dirt and poverty of the surrounding neighborhood."

Nathaniel Hawthorne described the typical gin palace scene: "Ragged children come thither with old shaving-mugs. . . . Inconceivably sluttish women enter at noonday and stand at the counter among boon companions of both sexes, stirring up misery and jollity in a bumper together, and quaffing off the mixture with a relish. As for the men, they lounge there continually, drinking till they are drunken—drinking as long as they have a half-penny left—and then, as it seemed to me, waiting for a sixpenny miracle to be wrought in their pockets so as to enable them to be drunken again."

Just like Vegas.

What's in a Name?

During gin's heavily bootlegged history, it's acquired plenty of nicknames, and the list reads like a poetic inventory of the effects of inebriation: Madame Geneva, Blue Ruin, Blue Lightning, Strip-and-Go-Naked, Max, Partiality, Flashes of Lightning, South Sea Mountain, The Last Shift, Poverty, White Satin, Vinegar, Gossip, Crank(!), Mexico, Sky Blue, Cuckold's Comfort, Royal Poverty, My Lady's Eye-water, Kill-Grief, Cock-my-Cap, King Theodore of Corsica, Red Eye, Tow-row, The Cream of the Valley, Knock-Me-Down, The Out-and-Out, No Mistake, The Celebrated Butter Gun [God, I wish I knew the story behind that one], The Regular Flare-up, Cholic Water, Make Shift, Lush, Forty Rod, Phlegm Cutter, and, last but not least, Bob.

Squib Kicked

The British Temperance Movement wasn't very successful. One bishop in the House of Lords declared that he would "prefer to see all England free better than England sober." But one thing it did get banned was the "squib." This was the child-sized measurement of gin sold to ten-year-olds by disreputable landlords.

USEFUL INFO

The Flavors in Gin

Juniper is still used for flavoring, but modern gin also incorporates botanicals like cinnamon, coriander, caraway seeds, orrisroot, orange and lemon peel, fennel, bitter almonds, and cardamom.

If you want to try sussing these flavors out for yourself, here's a good trick: Cover the glass with the palm of your hand and give it a few gentle swirls. Then take your hand off and sniff the glass. The swirling helps release the gin's fragrance.

"London Dry"

This term stems from the gin craze when bootleg gin was heavily sweetened to make it drinkable. Quality gin makers used the term "London Dry" to differentiate their stuff from the poor man's drink. It no longer has any real meaning.

Golden Gin

Modern Dutch "genever," or "golden gin," is very different from English gin. It has much more character and flavor, befitting the Dutch practice of drinking it straight like schnapps. Unlike other gins, Dutch gins are also usually barrel-aged for one to three years, during which it acquires a pale golden color.

Dorothy Parker

(1893–1967)

Dorothy Parker, the quintessential New Yorker, was actually a Jersey girl named Dorothy Rothschild. But she moved to Manhattan at the age of twenty after the deaths of her brother (who went down on the *Titanic*) and her father. She earned her keep as a piano player at a dance studio, but in her spare time she began writing.

Her ability to turn a phrase soon got her hired at *Vanity Fair* as New York's only female drama critic. She quickly became a legend in literary circles for her acid-tongued criticism and merciless wit. She also gained a reputation for her love of Johnnie Walker straight, high-end prescription pills, and libertine sex. As to the impact of these vices on her career, she declared, "Salary is no object: I want only enough to keep body and soul apart."

This sort of intellectual-slacker attitude earned her an invitation to a drinking club that formed at the Algonquin Hotel in 1919. The Round Table was dedicated to the pursuit of two things—drink and witty conversation. It was comprised of New York's most famous critics and conversationalists—James Thurber, Robert Benchley, George Kaufman,

Ring Lardner, Alexander Woollcott, Noël Coward and, paradoxically enough, the silent Marx Brother, Harpo. Dorothy was the only female member, but over the next decade, she emerged as the ringleader of this merry and merciless band.

The Algonquin Round Table gained nationwide notoriety as newspaper gossip columns breathlessly reported the bons mots minted on those boozy afternoons:

DOROTHY PARKER:

"Three be the things I shall never attain: envy, content and sufficient champagne."

"That woman speaks eighteen languages and can't say 'no' in any of them."

"Brevity is the soul of lingerie."

"If you laid all the girls of Vassar end to end, I wouldn't be surprised."

ROBERT BENCHLEY:

"I know I'm drinking myself to a slow death, but then I'm in no hurry."

"Drinking makes such fools of people, and people are such fools to begin with it's just compounding the felony."

ALEXANDER WOOLLCOTT:

"All the things I really like are either immoral, illegal or fattening."

OSCAR LEVANT:

"I don't drink; I don't like it—it makes me feel good."

HARPO MARX:

<Honk!>

And the most famous quote attributed to pretty much every member of the Round Table: "I must get out of these wet clothes and into a dry martini" (for the story behind this quote see page 153).

Actually, Parker's wit was honed a little too sharply at the Algonquin. She was fired from *Vanity Fair* after her reviews became too sarcastic to print. But she went on to bigger pastures—she helped start *The New Yorker*; she moved to Paris, where she befriended and influenced the young Ernest Hemingway; she moved to Hollywood, where she won an Oscar for the screenplay of *A Star Is Born* (1937).

Things came to a crashing halt, though, when she was blacklisted by a Commie-obsessed Hollywood after refusing to name names. With her career torpedoed, she spent the rest of her life struggling with marriages (three) and her drinking, which she unsuccessfully (though ingeniously) tried to decrease by adding soda water to her whiskey.

After her death in 1967, she proved to be just as feisty as she was in life, leaving her entire estate to the NAACP and this epitaph on her gravestone: *"Excuse my dust."*

VODKA

"Sparks! They fly from your stomach to the furthest reaches of your body." —ANTON CHEKHOV

Vodka is the king of the cocktail. It's America's number-one-selling spirit, accounting for 20 percent of all alcohol sold, and is estimated to be in one out of every four drinks served in the world. But the first reference to it as a mixer only came in 1930, in the *Savoy Cocktail Book,* where the reader is instructed to "shake well, strain into a cocktail glass and tossitoff quickski."

Nowadays, it's behind every bar, but before the 1930s, vodka was confined to the remote, frozen expanses of Russia, Poland, and Scandinavia. And each of these countries proudly pounds its chest proclaiming vodka as its own invention, which is why it's fairly amusing to learn that it actually came from Italy.

Well, Morocco actually. Probably around A.D. 800. But Genoese traders brought it to Italy in the thirteenth century, where it was jealously guarded by physicians and clergy for the next hundred years. Then, the Genoese merchants decided to kick-start trade a little and introduce this clear spirit to new markets. They went east.

In the late-fourteenth century, Russia got its first taste of this thing they called *zhizennia voda*, "water of life." It was love at first sight. In fact, after a few centuries of drinking, they got a little misty-eyed (as drinkers are prone to do), and in the mid-1700s started referring to it affectionately as "dear little water," or *vodka*.

> "VODKA IS ONLY DRUNK FOR ONE REASON, AND IF YOU HAVE A BOTTLE OF VODKA YOU'LL ALWAYS FIND A REASON."
> —RUSSIAN SAYING

Like the Italians, the clergy latched onto it first. During Russian religious ceremonies, vodka was passed to the congregation in cups—*gallon*-sized cups. And whoever declined was considered impious, and also, a big wuss.

Eastern distillation was still pretty crude, though, and it was common practice to add herbs and spices to mask the harsh flavors left over. But when Peter the Great took the throne in 1689, he was keen to westernize the court. By making it more familiar to Europe, he hoped to expand Russia's marketplace for the drink he pitched as "the aunt of wine."

To glean the secrets of the West, he decided he should travel through Europe. Incognito. The only drawbacks to this were: his Russian accent, his uncontrollable facial tic and arm flail, and the fact that he was 6'8", which by the standards of the time meant he looked like Shaquille O'Neal.

So Dutch gin makers weren't exactly bamboozled by this spastic Russian Shaq who kept hanging around and asking questions, all the while insisting that no, no, he really *wasn't* the czar of Russia. Nonetheless, they explained their advanced distilling techniques, which he then brought back to Russia.

After that, vodka progressed in leaps and bounds over the next hundred years, as producers were able to purify vodka into the clear and flavorless (relatively speaking) drink we recognize today.

Vodka's big advantage as a drink is that it can come from virtually any base product. All that purifying leeches out any original flavors, which makes it very convenient for peasants—Poles could use potatoes or wheat; Scandinavians could use barley. In fact, vodka making was one of the everyday chores of any Swedish farmwife (until King Gustav III banned home brewing in favor of national distilleries, which he owned, natch).

In czarist Russia, it was a different story. Peasants didn't own the land, the gentry did. So each lord developed his own vodka from the grains harvested on his estates, which he then sold in the local tavern (which he also owned) back to the peasants, who reaped the grain that made the vodka in the first place. In other words, being a commoner in czarist Russia was a major-league screw-job. So they did something about it.

"THERE CANNOT BE NOT ENOUGH SNACKS,
THERE CAN ONLY BE NOT ENOUGH VODKA.
THERE CAN BE NO SILLY JOKES,
THERE CAN ONLY BE NOT ENOUGH VODKA.
THERE CAN BE NO UGLY WOMEN,
THERE CAN ONLY BE NOT ENOUGH VODKA.
THERE CANNOT BE TOO MUCH VODKA,
THERE CAN ONLY BE NOT ENOUGH VODKA."

—RUSSIAN SAYING

The Russian Revolution in 1917 overthrew the czar, and vodka, too, for a while. Lenin was a rabid tee-totaler. So much so that he decided to have the aristo-cratic Smirnoff family killed because of its title as the official vodka maker to the czar. Only one son, Vladimir, survived, and that was by chance. He was awaiting execution when a raid on the prison allowed him to escape. He fled to Paris, taking the family recipe with him.

As an émigré, Vladimir had a hard time getting the family business back on its feet. So, in 1934, he sold the American rights to Rudolph Kunett (whose name sounded slightly more vodka-y in its pre–Ellis Island form, Kunetchansky). But Rudolph had a tough time of it. No one in the States had ever really heard of vodka. He eventually gave in and sold the Smirnoff name in 1939 for $14,000, which in '39 dollars doesn't seem like such a bad deal until you consider that Smirnoff's worth a few billion now.

The company that bought it then made a very smart decision. Like TiVo, sushi, and LSD, most Amer-ican fads start in California, even back then. So they teamed up with the owner of a British pub in LA, the Cock and Bull, who was trying to start a fad for ginger ale. It wasn't working. But with his unsold bottles, they created the first cocktail-as-marketing-tool—the Moscow Mule (vodka, ginger ale, and a slice of lime).

The Moscow Mule became chic. The recently in-vented Bloody Mary became chic. And chic-est of all, vodka became the drink of forties film stars, the main theory being that they could get silently smashed on film sets without the smell alerting studio spies (as bourbon was known to do).

Perhaps that's why Smirnoff came out with the slo-gan: "Smirnoff leaves you breathless." Thus becoming the first (and possibly only) drink that promoted itself as a way to get loaded at lunch without alerting your boss. But it worked. Like no other ad campaign before or since.

In 1950, vodka sold forty thousand cases in the

United States. In 1954, it sold 1.1 million. And with the advent of the vodka martini in '55, 4.4 million. In '67, it outsold gin. In '76, it beat whiskey.

America may have claimed victory in the Cold War, but Russia has claimed our livers ever since.

USELESS INFO

How Peter Got Great

When he was feeling magnanimous, Peter the Great would ride through villages on a bear-drawn sleigh tossing bottles of vodka to the peasants.

A Barrel of Life

In the sixteenth century, a tradition began among Polish and Russian gentry to celebrate the birth of a child. The parents would fill empty wine barrels with vodka and leave them untouched until the day of the child's wedding, whereupon the barrel-aged vodka would be used to toast the happy couple.

Russian Rain

Russian superstition maintains that the corpse of a man who dies while drinking vodka can be tossed into a bog to make it rain.

Crazy Russian Love

Whether they're patriotic or just have a drinking problem, Russians have a pretty intense relationship with their national drink. In the 1800s, vodka accounted for 40 percent of Russia's income! In the Soviet era, it accounted for 15 to 20 percent of all retail sales, and taxes on vodka funded the original cosmonaut program. In the mid-1990s, annual consumption was thirty-eight liters for every man, woman, and child!

Water Wars

Water is the key ingredient in vodka. The purer, the better. So it's no surprise that top-shelf vodkas compete for the unofficial title of Strangest Water Source: One Finnish vodka claims it's made with water from the Ice Age, a deep well that taps an underground reservoir carved by the glaciers. A Danish vodka beats that by claiming its water is from the glaciers themselves, chipped away from ice caps in Greenland.

USEFUL INFO

Ice, Cold, Winter

Vodka is a no-brainer to store and serve. Store in a freezer; serve ice-cold. In fact, this was part of the reason vodka thrived in the north and east. Since it doesn't freeze, it could be transported on slow-moving carts in the harsh winters without fear of cracking its containers.

A Tasting Trick

Here's a neat Russian tradition: immediately after downing a shot of vodka, sniff a slice of black bread—the aromas will mingle and complement each other.

East versus West

Vodka is split between two schools—the Eastern tradition of drinking it as straight shots and the Western use of it as a mixer. The former prizes vodka with character, while the latter requires that it be as neutral as possible. Thus:

- Polish vodka probably has the greatest range, with taste and texture highly prized and a long tradition of flavorings (bison grass, fruit, etc.).

- Russian vodkas are usually a bit oilier (they feel buttery in the mouth) and are not quite as sweet as Polish vodka.

- Western vodkas (including Scandinavian vodkas like Absolut that are geared toward the Western market) tend to be highly filtered, crisp, and less flavorful.

"VODKA IS TASTELESS GOING DOWN, BUT IT IS MEMORABLE COMING UP."
–GARRISON KEILLOR

BRANDY

THE ALCHEMIST'S ESSENCE

"Claret is the liquor for boys; port for men; but he who aspires to be a hero must drink brandy."
—SAMUEL JOHNSON

Brandy is the oldest of the distilled liquors. Only at first it wasn't a liquor, it was medicine. When the Moors invaded Spain in the eighth century, they were distilling everything in a search for new medicines (see page 77). So they turned their attention to the local wine and distilled it to its most concentrated essence. But when they left, this wine-liquor left with them. The Spanish forgot all about the invaders' medicine. Fortunately, not everyone did.

A few monasteries continued distilling wine, and by the late-thirteenth century, its medicinal qualities came to the attention of the papal doctor, who prescribed it to three different popes as a means of prolonging life. By the fourteenth century, the pope's health drink became so popular, and began generating so much tax revenue, that the Romans had to give it a name just for bookkeeping purposes—*geprantwein*, ("burned wine").

To the Dutch traders working in southern Europe, this stuff was a gold mine. It was Tang for the fourteenth century. Wine reduced to its essence. In their minds, it would take up a fraction of the cargo space of wine at a fraction of the cost. And when they arrived at another city, they could simply add water and sell it as normal wine with *much* better profits.

Calling it *brandewijn* (Dutch for "burned wine"), they began shipping it abroad. But the traders had a pleasant surprise waiting for them. *Brandewijn* tasted better at the end of these trips than at the beginning. Early brandy was harsh stuff, akin to moonshine, because people drank the clear fluid straight off the still. But in transit, the wooden casks that held the *brandewijn* were mellowing the harsh flavors and creating something that wasn't just boiled-down wine.

The Dutch quickly traveled Europe to spread the booze and search for new areas of production: Germany, England (where *brandewijn* got anglicized into "brandy wine"), and one particular port on the west coast of France.

Lying just to the north of Bordeaux's famous wine country, the Cognac region's wines had always been the ugly duckling by comparison—sharp, flavorless, and, the most unforgivable sin, low in alcohol. The one thing the area had going for it was a seaport large enough for heavy trading ships. So it was by pure chance, really, that the Dutch set their stills up there. And it was by chance they discovered that the same qualities in grapes that made stinky wine made for stellar brandy.

COGNAC

"Good cognac is like a woman. Do not assault it. Coddle and warm it in your hands before you sip it."
—WINSTON CHURCHILL

In the same way that champagne is sparkling wine from the Champagne region of France, cognac is brandy from the Cognac region. And, like Champagne, Cognac perfected the art form.

Why? The legend goes that in the sixteenth century, a knight by the name of Jacques de la Croix-Maron had a nightmare in which Satan tried boiling him to get his soul. When that didn't work, Satan, with a plucky can-do attitude, tried to boil him again. The knight bolted awake with the secret to getting at cognac's soul—*double* distillation, a process that removes impurities and makes a drink smoother.

And if getting cooking tips from Satan sounds a little, you know, *insane*, it doesn't make any of Cognaçois blink twice. Everything about that region is a little bit . . . off. The trains don't run out there. The rooftops are blighted and black with mold. There's something in the air that does it. Literally.

> "BRANDY, n. A cordial composed of one part THUNDER-AND-LIGHTNING, one part REMORSE, TWO PARTS BLOODY MURDER, one part DEATH-HELL-AND-THE-GRAVE and four PARTS CLARIFIED SATAN."—AMBROSE BIERCE

It's known as "The Angel's Share," the evaporation from cognac as it ages in barrels—74,000 bottles of cognac *a day* waft into the air. Hence, the mold. It's a unique variety that feeds on cognac fumes. That's right, there's alcoholic *mold* (albeit with very classy taste). And tracks were never allowed to go through the nearby countryside for fear the sparks from a passing train would ignite the fumes and torch entire vineyards.

Cognac may owe its inception to Satan, but it owes its smooth finish (and all those fumes) to war. Specifically, the War of Spanish Succession. Brandy makers knew from the Dutch that wood aging helped, but no one knew how much until the war halted trade with

England in 1701. Merchants stored their excess brandy in barrels, and when the conflict ended twelve years later, the brandy emerged with a mellow, golden flavor.

Customers quickly latched onto cognac as something special (though Armagnac also has its fans). Big money rolled in, and so rose the big houses: Martell (founded by a former smuggler), Hennessy (an Irish soldier of fortune), Courvoisier, and Rémy Martin.

Together, they account for four-fifths of all cognac exports. And, together, they've been responsible for the decline in cognac's fortunes. It's one of the few instances in modern times where the Wal-Mart ethos of "bigger is better" hasn't worked. The big houses wanted to protect their brand; they stuck to their rigid house styles. So drinkers turned to Scotch (see "Whiskey," page 86), which is cheaper anyway (for the simple reason that barley is cheaper to grow than grapes), and cognac turned into an old man's drink.

But recently, cognac's story has turned into something out of a college spring break movie. Now this is a fantastic metaphor, so follow me on this:

Cognac had become the fuddy-dud dean, out of touch and unpopular. But then a brash new student arrives on campus with his rebellious ways and his loud music. The student is Busta Rhymes with the rap song "Pass the Courvoisier." At first the dean is skeptical, but sales take off in the inner cities and suddenly Dean Cognac realizes that he's been too uptight for too long. And in the climactic scene, Dean Cognac sports shades and a do-rag and performs "Pass the Courvoisier" ("Everybody singing now . . .") in front of the wary trustees until they, too, succumb to the righteous rhythms and begin booty-dancing wildly as we freeze-frame on Busta Rhymes and Dean Cognac exchanging high-fives knowing that they—truly—have begun to "party hearty." Roll credits.

All right, well, the metaphor breaks down a little at the end there. For instance, I'm not sure whom the trustees represent (the grape growers, maybe?), but the point is that that one hit rap song has pulled cognac kicking and screaming out of the senior citizens, home and into the twenty-first century.

POMACE BRANDY

In Italy, it's *grappa;* in France, it's *marc;* in Spain, *aguardiente;* in Portugal, *bagaceira.* In fact, in every Old World wine-growing country, there's a peasant tradition of pomace brandy.

It can be thought of as the pig's feet of alcohol—the leftovers from something better. And that's what "pomace" is—the skins, pulps, and pits left over from grapes after they've been pressed for wine. And like pig's feet, pomace brandy is also pungent and *definitely* an acquired taste. But pretty good once you've acquired it.

> "SUITABLE ONLY FOR DEFROCKED PRIESTS, UNEMPLOYED BOOKKEEPERS AND HUSBANDS THAT HAVE BEEN CUCKOLDED."
>
> —ITALO CALVINO, WRITER

It dates far back into history, but the first record of it is from the fifteenth century. Back then, grape farmers couldn't afford to buy the very wines they were helping to produce. So ever-resourceful, they added water to the leftover pomace and distilled it. In northern Italy at harvesttime, *grappa* makers would travel from town to town with portable stills and set up right in the fields.

Recently, the drink has achieved some status, as it's now made with premium single-grape varieties and marketed to upscale wine enthusiasts as a way of truly understanding the essence of a particular grape and blah blah blah. But it's also still produced on very small scales by and for the locals of vineyards all over Europe, retaining its roots with peasants and pig's feet.

> "A KICK IN THE STOMACH TO GET . . . STARTED ON BAD MORNINGS."
>
> —GEORGE ORWELL

FRUIT BRANDY

Brandy's "burned wine" origins imply it can only be made with distilled grapes. But brandy is used as a catch-all phrase—along with eau-de-vie ("water of life")—to describe any distilled fruit essence. Thus, fruit brandies range wildly from France's incredible Calvados (apple) and framboise (raspberry) to the undrinkable slivovitz (plum). And no offense is meant to the fine, proud, genocidal people of former Yugoslavia, but their national drink tastes exactly how it sounds—slivovitz—like a diseased lizard slithering over your tongue.

USELESS INFO

"Paradise"

The name for the cellar where the oldest brandies in a cognac warehouse are stored.

Hair Care

Empress Elizabeth of Austria had famous floor-length hair, which she kept manageable and bouncy with a shampoo made from egg yolk, pressed onions, and twenty bottles of the finest French brandy.

Express Counter

Brandy was so popular in England that Dutch traders had to set up sales counters right on their boats to service the people clamoring on the docks for the newest shipments.

A Smuggled Tug of War

Eighteenth-century English smugglers used to sink kegs of brandy in the ocean, where they could be easily retrieved. One such drop was discovered in 1720, when local fishermen reeled in twenty-three kegs. Their luck was short-lived, though. Federal officers seized the kegs in the name of the Crown. The local lord of the town fought back by reseizing the brandy for the villagers. Royal officers then tried to re-reseize the brandy, but this time were rebuffed by an unruly mob. Finally, the army had to be called in to quell the rebellion and reclaim the kegs (which by then were somewhat drained).

USEFUL INFO

Tasting Tips

Tasting cognac's a little different from tasting wine. With cognac, the smell and aftertaste are the primary pursuits. The liquid is too strong to keep on your tongue for very long, so let it roll down your throat, then appreciate the aftertaste while you sniff the fumes. If you care.

The Brandy Code

Each brandy is described on the label by a series of letters:

E = extra
F = fine
M = mellow
O = old
P = pale
S = superior
V = very
X = extra

Unlike most liquors, these label designations aren't legally binding:

- AC: Aged two years, minimum.

- VS: Aged three to five years, sometimes called "three star."

- VSOP: Aged four to fifteen years, sometimes called "five star."

- XO: Aged six to twenty-plus years, given a variety of names like "reserve" or "luxury."

Champagne Brandy

With cognac, the word "champagne" has nothing to do with bubbly. It means "an open stretch of land," and in Cognac country there are two: Petite Champagne and Grande Champagne. Both produce premium cognac, but Grande is considered better.

- For a bottle to be labeled "Fine Champagne," at least 60 percent must come from the Grande region.

- To be labeled "Grand Fine Champagne," 100 percent must come from Grande.

A Word of Warning

For all the hoo-ha over cognac, it can be a bit of a rip-off. High-end cognac is *incredibly* expensive, but even for experienced drinkers, it can be hard to differentiate from some mid-level whiskeys. Try this blind taste test: Martell's Gordon Bleu ($150 a bottle) versus Glenlivet ($40).

"EDWIN LAW TOLD ME AN INFALLIBLE RECEIPT FOR WARMING COLD AND WET FEET ON A JOURNEY. POUR HALF A GLASS OF BRANDY INTO EACH BOOT. . . . HE HAS BEEN A LONG TIME IN NOVA SCOTIA."

—REV. FRANCIS KILVERT

TEQUILA

CONQUISTADORS, BANDITOS, MARIACHIS, OH MY!

"Tequila, scorpion honey, harsh dew of the doglands, essence of Aztec, crème de cacti; tequila, oily and thermal like the sun in solution . . . tequila, savage water of sorcery, what confusion and mischief your sly rebellious drops do generate." —TOM ROBBINS

The blue agave. Grown on the slopes of an extinct volcano. Pollinated at night by bats. Spikes that grow up to seven feet tall. Discovered by Aztecs. Distilled by conquistadors. Even if it didn't have its association with bandoleer-wearing bandits, the drink made out of this plant was bound to be one tough hombre.

Spanish troops stumbled across it in 1521, when they arrived in Mexico and found themselves facing a serious problem—sobriety. They'd sailed over with a large stock of brandy and wine, but they were quickly running out and conquistadoring is thirsty work. Raping and pillaging just isn't the same if you're sober.

Desperate to avoid this looming crisis, the Spaniards tried something the locals had been brewing for at least three thousand years—pulque, a milky beverage fermented from the agave plant.

The agave was as sacred to the Aztecs as the buffalo

was to the North American Indians. It was a godsend, literally, that was incorporated into every aspect of their culture as food, clothing, rope, and paper. And then, one day, so the legend goes, a lightning bolt struck the heart of the agave and was transformed into the alcoholic sap that came oozing out (see "Tepoztecal," page 191).

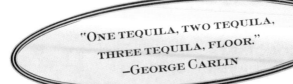

"ONE TEQUILA, TWO TEQUILA, THREE TEQUILA, FLOOR."
—GEORGE CARLIN

The Aztecs thought this liquid lightning was yet another gift from the gods. The Spaniards had a different reaction. They thought it sucked. But they brought something with them from the Old World that they thought could improve the taste—the art of distilling.

So the conquistadors hacked away the spikes to get at the agave's heart (which looks like a pineapple and weighs eighty to two hundred pounds), then roasted, mashed, fermented, and distilled it, and out came a fiery liquid they called mescal. That's mescal, not tequila. Tequila is to mescal the way cognac is to brandy or Scotch is to whiskey. It's a specific style of the drink from a specific region. In tequila's case, the region is the state of Jalisco, in which there's a small farming town nestled at the base of a volcano named Tequila.

The word *tequila* means "the place of harvesting plants," and the locals had an ancient tradition of cultivating the best and most bountiful agave. So it was there that the first commercial distillery was established in 1600.

Tequila didn't immediately take Mexico by storm. Like any new liquor, it had to fight against centuries of ingrained habits: the aristocrats of Spanish descent drank European wine and the indigenous Indian population drank pulque. Plus, this new drink from Jalisco had a bit of a bad reputation from the very beginning, because Jalisco was also bandit country.

When the conquistadors invaded Mexico, most of the country fell within the first year. But the people of Jalisco were proud descendants of Aztec warriors and they held the Spanish at bay for twenty years. The region had been a source of rebellions and uprising ever since, so when the Mexican Revolution touched off in 1910, Jalisco became a major battleground.

Rebels and army regiments fought back and forth across the state, and to fuel their fighting spirit, they commandeered every distillery along the way. Tequila became "the drink of the trenches," indelibly stamped with the image of bandoleered revolutionaries fighting for the people. The only problem was, the people didn't know about it . . . until the movies told them.

> "HEY, PASS THE PENICILLIN."
> —PEDRO INFANTE ASKING HIS SERVANT FOR A BOTTLE OF TEQUILA IN THE FILM *LOS TRES GARCÍAS*.

When the dust settled in the 1920s, the entire country was drinking less than 160,000 gallons of tequila a year. Mexico was a nation with an identity crisis. They'd finally thrown off their Spanish yoke, but they were no longer Indians. So who were they? The answer came in the 1940s, when Mexican cinema entered its "golden age." The studios wanted to make movies that were uniquely Mexican, so they looked to rebellious Jalisco and its two greatest traditions—tequila and the mariachi.

Moviegoers quickly learned that *real* Mexicans—singing cowboys, revolutionaries, and ranchers—drank the drink of Mexico. They drank tequila.

Despite the fact that the rebels had smashed and

grabbed most of their inventory during the Revolution, distillers knew a good marketing strategy when they saw one. Bottles of tequila began sporting pictures and names of famous bandits (even Pancho Villa's horse, Siete Leguas, got his own brand). Mexican consumption soared and tequila became a symbol of national pride.

The international community, however (and America in particular), was still wary of this upstart country and its feisty drink. That is, until the exotic cocktail craze of the 1950s, when it was formally introduced to Mexico's most charming ambassador—the margarita. Disguised inside ice and fruit juice, tequila slipped across the border into America, where it was embraced with open arms.

Sales skyrocketed, and from there, it was a short step to where tequila is today. Besides the industrial high-end stuff, sipping tequilas has been developed for connoisseurs. Prices have jumped accordingly, but that's not the only reason.

In the mid-1990s, the El Niño weather pattern wiped out the agave crops, which take eight to twelve years to grow. The remaining plants became so valuable that Jalisco has experienced a new crime wave. Marauders have been hijacking the agave out of the fields in the dead of night. Tradition dies hard; tequila hasn't totally abandoned its bandit ways.

USELESS INFO

Tequileras

This is the name for a tequila distillery, but in many parts of Mexico it's also the description for a cold, overcast afternoon. "Tequileras" weather is traditionally coped with by staying at home and drinking *añejo* with friends and music.

The Worm

Actually, it's not in tequila, and it's not a worm. It's in mescal, and it's a butterfly caterpillar that is found in the heart of the agave plant. It was known to improve the flavor of mescal, and in the 1950s, a distributor in Mexico City decided to include one in every bottle as a marketing ploy. Others soon followed suit, and the "worm" took on another use, as a proof of potency. If it was decayed at all inside the bottle, the tequila had been watered down.

Margarita

There is much debate over who invented the margarita. The ingredients first appeared together in a British book of drink recipes. But according to Mexico's Ministry of Tequila (yes, that's a real government agency), the strongest candidate was Francisco "Pancho" Morales on July 4, 1942, in Tommy's Bar.

The legend goes that a woman walked into the bar and asked for a drink Morales had never heard of. Like any bartender, he bluffed, and made up something on the spot involving tequila, ice, Cointreau, fruit juice, and *voilà*! The margarita was born. But apparently, Morales never liked his own concoction very much. In fact, he left bartending altogether. He moved to the United States and became a milkman for the rest of his life.

USEFUL INFO

Types of Tequila

The four basic types of tequila:

JOVEN/SUAVE (YOUNG/SMOOTH): A mixture of 51 percent agave and 49 percent other sugars. Aged less than two months.

PLATA/BLANCO (SILVER/WHITE): Bottled without any aging, which accounts for its clear color. No aging means no outside flavors, so it's considered the "purest" tequila.

REPOSADO (RESTED, ALSO LABELED AS GOLD): Barrel-aged for two months to one year, which gives it a golden color. This is the most popular tequila.

AÑEJO (AGED): Usually 100 percent agave (this is specified on the label by law). Aged for one to five years. Producers sometimes use whiskey or cognac barrels for flavor. Dark and smooth, it's considered the most sophisticated tequila.

When Tequila Isn't Tequila

When tequila is not 100 percent agave (and most aren't), the remainder is alcohol distilled from sugarcane. In other words, rum.

The String of Pearls

A test of high-quality tequila is to swirl it in your glass for a minute. Small bubbles will appear and rise to the sides, forming a necklace of pearls around the glass. If there are no bubbles, or the bubbles disappear quickly, the tequila is of poor quality or has been watered down.

COCKTAILS

BASTARD CHILD OF THE JAZZ AGE

"Do not allow children to mix drinks. It is unseemly and they use too much vermouth." —STEVE ALLEN

Along with Western movies, jazz, and the Empire State Building, cocktails are considered a quintessentially American invention. But why is that? As long as there have been drinks, there have been mixed drinks.

Early alcohol wasn't the purest stuff, so all sorts of methods were invented to improve the taste. The second-century Roman emperor Lucius Aelius Aurelius Commodus was known to enjoy lemon juice and powdered viper in his wine.

By the seventeenth century, punch (rum or wine with spirits, fruit, and spices) was already a well-honed art. And, like cocktails, every mixture was assigned a funky name like the Bishop, the Devil's Toothbrush (see page 205), and Huckle-My-Butt, which inspired such ditties as this:

"Huckle-My-Butt, Huckle-My-Butt,
It is welcome alike both in palace and hut,
Should I have fifty children, each rogue and each slut,
All shall be christened Huckle-My-Butt."
—ANONYMOUS

Punch was a party drink, and as such, it tended to be drunk communally out of one large loving cup, which was passed around and around the table until it could be passed no more. But by the start of the nineteenth century, people gave up drinking out of buckets and went for the individual serving. This allowed mixed drinks to be tailored for more personal use.

Americans, for instance, decided to have it for breakfast. No, seriously. When the word "cocktail" first appeared in print in 1806, it was described as a breakfast drink made up of "spirits of any kind, sugar, water, and bitters." This gave America all the sugar and alcohol it needed to get up and go-go-go. And while these early cocktails weren't *quite* what we consider to be a cocktail today (i.e., a mixture of several liquors), they were getting close. The real leap forward came with vermouth (see page 157).

> "COCKTAIL LOUNGES ARE USUALLY HALF-LIT TO MATCH THE PATRONS."
> —ANONYMOUS

Bartenders quickly realized that vermouth's multi-faceted flavors made it the diplomat of alcohol. It softened the harsh edges of some liquors, and allowed others with opposing tastes to coexist in the same glass. And once ice became commercially available in the 1830s, all the ingredients for cocktails were in place.

But, again, why did *America* become the cocktail nation? Why not England? They're a bunch of drunks. They had ice and vermouth. They even put out the first bartender's guide (the rakishly titled *The Bon Vivant's Guide, or How to Mix Cocktails*, 1862). So why America?

Because . . . England had cocktails, but they also had beer, wine, and other legal liquor to choose from.

America didn't. On January 16, 1920, it had Prohibition.

And that's when the party started. The Jazz Age hit the stage. Flappers started flapping; gun molls flashed their gams. The 1920s roared into life, and the fuel it ran on was cocktails. Because simply put, bootlegged liquor sucked.

Rum and whiskey were smuggled over the borders, but the main liquor of prohibition was the drink the moonshiners could moonshine most easily—gin (for an explanation, see "Gin," page 115). But bathtub gin was deadly stuff, sometimes literally—industrial alcohol cut with glycerine and tap water. The only way to cover the awful taste was to add fruit juice, vermouth, any other liquor on hand, and create a cocktail.

Everyone in America quickly earned their Ph.D. in mixology. Suddenly, inventing new cocktails joined baseball as the national sport, and by 1929, bartender's manuals officially recognized over 120 distinct recipes.

But while the hoi polloi escaped Prohibition by holding their nose and swallowing quickly, rich Americans escaped Prohibition in style. They traveled to other countries. And they took two things with them— money and a taste for cocktails.

The grand hotel bars of Europe were forced to cater to this crass new demand of their American guests, but not without the requisite bitching. One French culinary guide at the time described cocktails as something "to make a shark retch or a crocodile vomit." And the French poet/author/professional crank Paul Claudel went a bit overboard when he said, "A cocktail is to a glass of wine as rape is to love."

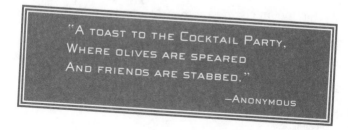

"A TOAST TO THE COCKTAIL PARTY,
WHERE OLIVES ARE SPEARED
AND FRIENDS ARE STABBED."

—ANONYMOUS

Nonetheless, no one could deny the fact that the Jazz Age ex-pats looked as if they were having a blast. And eventually, even the most hard-hearted of critics relented and recognized the genius of the drink that led the charge of cocktails into every bar in the world. The drink described by Soviet premier Nikita Khrushchev as "America's secret weapon"—the martini.

MARTINI
(aka "The Silver Bullet")

"The only American invention as perfect as a sonnet."
—H. L. MENCKEN

"I'm not talking a cup of cheap gin splashed over an ice cube. I'm talking satin, fire and ice; Fred Astaire in a glass; surgical cleanliness; insight and comfort; redemption and absolution. I'm talking a Martini."
—ANONYMOUS

Why does the martini get its own section? Because it's the Mount Everest of mixology, the most beloved, most culturally influential cocktail of all time.

The first recorded rumblings of the martini were in 1862, in *The Bon Vivant's Guide*, with a recipe for the Gin Cocktail. By 1884, the same recipe appeared in another bartender's guide, only this time under the name Martinez.

Where the name "martini" came from has been a source of hot debate by amateur cocktail scholars with *way* too much time on their hands. They attribute it to everything from a gold miner, a British army rifle, and the town of Martinez, California, to an Italian bartender, the Rockefellers, and the Martini & Rossi vermouth company. Each of these explanations has been labeled absurd by the opposing camps, leaving no one the wiser.

> "MARTINI IS JUST A LONGER WORD FOR JOY." —CLARA BOW

Either way, you'd hardly recognize the martini in its original form. It was a 1:1 mixture of gin and vermouth. But as the quality of gin improved and tastes ran toward drier cocktails, that ratio has slowly moved toward the point where martini enthusiasts compete for the most creative way in which to ignore the vermouth altogether.

Some whisper the word "vermouth" over the martini. Winston Churchill would simply glance at the vermouth on the other side of the room. But possibly the best idea comes from the Spanish film director Luis Buñuel, who suggests "allowing a ray of sunlight to shine through a bottle of Noilly Prat [vermouth] before it hits the bottle of gin. . . . A dry martini should resemble the Immaculate Conception, for, as Saint Thomas Aquinas once noted, the generative power of the Holy Ghost pierced the Virgin's hymen 'like a ray of sunlight through a window—leaving it unbroken.' "

"I Must Get Out of These Wet Clothes and into a Dry Martini"

This famous quote is the epitome of twitty wit. It has been attributed to any number of people, but most often to Robert Benchley, a member of the Algonquin Round Table (see "Dorothy Parker," page 124).

That's because Benchley delivered the line in the Ginger Rogers's film *The Major and the Minor* (1942). But the line appeared earlier in the Mae West film *Every Day's a Holiday* (1937), delivered by the actor Charles Butterworth. The screenplay was credited to

Mae West, so *Bartlett's* gives her the honors. However, she was notorious for stealing credits from writers.

Benchley, ever the gentleman, never took credit for the line. He steadfastly maintained that it came from Butterworth, who coined it one not-so-sober night after falling into the swimming pool at the Garden of Allah (a notoriously riotous Hollywood resort).

The Martini Shot

Slang term used by old-time studio film directors to describe the last shot of the day.

The Gibson

The Gibson, a martini with a cocktail onion instead of an olive, apparently came about in the 1890s. Charles Gibson, an artist famous for his fashionable magazine illustrations of young women known as "Gibson Girls," enjoyed meeting his friends for afternoon cocktails at the Players Club in Manhattan. But he needed to return to work with a clear head, so he came to an arrangement with the bartender.

The bartender put ice water in a martini glass for Gibson and marked it with a cocktail onion instead of an olive, leaving no one the wiser. But his friends liked the onion idea so much they began imitating it, thus queering Charles's ability to get away with sobriety, and creating a new drink in the process.

Helpful Hint for Staying Dry

For the perfect homemade dry martini, the bartender at the Ritz Hotel in London suggests opening a new bottle of gin and topping it off with vermouth. Then simply shake it well each time before pouring.

Mint Julep

"With the thermometer at 100 degrees, one of the most delightful and insinuating potations that was ever invented." —FREDERICK MARRYAT, NINETEENTH-CENTURY CAPTAIN IN ROYAL NAVY

The word "julep" comes from Persian for "rose water." It came into English in the fifteenth century as a description for a syrupy drink used to disguise the bad taste of medicine. But the first "mint julep" was poured sometime in the early eighteenth century, earning it the distinction as one of the first American drinks that could be considered a cocktail.

"THEY SAY THAT YOU MAY ALWAYS KNOW THE GRAVE OF A VIRGINIAN AS, FROM THE QUANTITY OF JULEP HE HAS DRUNK, MINT INVARIABLY SPRINGS UP WHERE HE HAS BEEN BURIED." —FREDERICK MARRYAT

As to where it first started, that's the sort of conversation that quickly leads to pistols at dawn. Every state below the Mason-Dixon line has a different recipe (boiling down to rye versus bourbon and crushing the mint versus leaving it unmolested), and like barbecue and beauty queens, each state claims theirs is the best. The name first appeared in print in 1803, described as a "dram of spirituous liquor that has mint in it, taken by Virginians in the morning."

Its popularity has since declined, but it's still revived on occasions when people want to invoke southern tradition and dress like Colonel Sanders. The central occasion is, of course, the Kentucky Derby, when Churchill Downs sells eighty thousand mint juleps in a single day.

"TO PLEASE KAY, THEY HAD STARTED HAVING COCKTAILS EVERY NIGHT IN THE ALUMINUM COCKTAIL SHAKER. THE DIFFERENCE BETWEEN THEM WAS THAT WHAT SHE LIKED WAS THE LITTLE FORMALITY AND WHAT HAROLD LIKED WAS THE LIQUOR."—MARY MCCARTHY, *THE GROUP*

The Manhattan

Reputedly invented in 1874 by a swinging American named Jennie Jerome, who would later marry and give birth to Winston Churchill (see page 212). It was first served during a party she hosted at the Manhattan Club in New York City, from which the drink eventually took its name.

Black Velvet

London, 1861: The gentlemen members of the Brooks Club were calling for their morning glass of champagne to clear the cobwebs from the night before. But the club steward decided that bubbly was too frivolous a drink, since the nation was still officially mourning the death of Prince Albert. So he threw a proverbial widow's veil over the champagne by mixing it with Guinness stout.

Rob Roy

The Rob Roy came about with the debut of the Broadway show *Rob Roy*, in 1894. Back then, it was a popular pastime to create a new drink in honor of every Broadway opening. But in this case, the bartender may have been a bit of a wise-ass.

Rob Roy, the show, was written by Henry Louis De Koven, a mediocre talent whose songs were famous for being thinly veiled rip-offs of famous works. *Robin Hood,* his box office hit in 1891, was dubbed *Robbin' Ludwig* by the critics.

Thus "Rob Roy," the drink, is a thinly veiled rip-off of a Manhattan, simply replacing the rye with Scotch in honor of the show's Highland hero.

Mai Tai

Created by "Trader Vic," one of the founding fathers of the Polynesian tiki lounge craze that hit America in the forties and fifties. He reportedly served his newest invention to two friends from Tahiti who described it as "*Maitai toa ae!,*" which in Tahitian means "Out of this world, the best!"

USELESS INFO

Vermouth

Though it's the linchpin in almost all major cocktails, less than 10 percent of the population actually knows what vermouth is, according to *Wine Spectator* magazine. Invented in Italy in the eighteenth century, vermouth is a liqueur—a fortified wine flavored with as many as fifty different berries, herbs, roots, and flowers—that takes up to a year to make.

The name comes from the German word *wermut,* or wormwood (of absinthe fame), which meant something like "manliness," because it was originally used as an aphrodisiac. Alternately, it was also used as a poison to rid a bed of fleas. Draw your own jokes. One early brand of French vermouth was named Gauloise. The drink has faded, but the infamously stinky French cigarettes named after it live on.

Highball

The general term for any liquor mixed in a tall glass with ice and a carbonated liquid. The phrase comes from early railroad workers who used the term "highball" as the signal to trains for "full speed ahead."

The Largest Cocktail Party Ever

In 1694, Admiral Edward Russell, commander of the British Mediterranean Fleet, threw a giant officers' party that employed a garden fountain as the punch bowl. The fountain was filled with 254 gallons of brandy, 250 gallons of Malaga wine, 1,200 pounds of sugar, 2,500 lemons, 20 gallons of lime juice, and 5 pounds of nutmeg. The bartenders rowed around in wooden canoes, filling up guests' cups and working in fifteen-minute shifts to avoid being overcome by the fumes and falling overboard.

The party went nonstop for a full week, only pausing briefly during rainstorms to erect a silk canopy over the punch to keep it from getting watered down. The party only ended when the fountain was drunk dry, literally; the bartenders' rowboats finally ran aground.

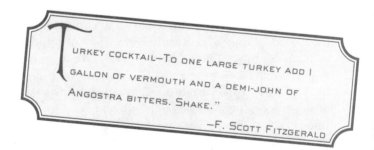

TURKEY COCKTAIL—To one large turkey add 1 gallon of vermouth and a demi-john of Angostra bitters. Shake."

—F. Scott Fitzgerald

"Cocktail": The Word, the Myth, the Legend

Like JFK conspiracy theories and the true identity of Jack the Ripper, the origin of the word "cocktail" is one of those glorious wormholes in history. Unencumbered by conclusive evidence, it's only constrained by the limits of the imagination. Here, then, are the top eleven most popular legends:

1. In the late 1700s in upstate New York, a barmaid named Betsy Flanagan served a customer a drink she'd garnished with some of the fighting-cock tail feathers that decorated the bar's walls.

2. The same Betsy Flanagan—popular girl—celebrated the American Revolution by stealing the chicken of a Tory farmer and serving it to American and French officers in her tavern, followed by drinks decorated with the tail feathers of the traitorous fowl.

3. A "cocked tail" was a British term for a racehorse of mixed origins (like a mixed drink, get it?), whose tail is bobbed to show his dubious pedigree.

4. During Mississippi's riverboat gambling days, the winner of duels was known as the "Cock of the Walk," and was honored in the bar with a drinking cup that resembled the breast of a cock, with a stirrer that resembled a tail feather.

5. The phrase "cock your tail" referred to a drink that would quickly knock you for a loop.

6. At some bar, somewhere, at some point in time, all the half-finished glasses at the end of the night were poured into a ceramic rooster with a tap in its tail. Stew bums could then buy a cheap shot of the resulting potent mix.

7. Around 1800, the king of Mexico and an unnamed American general were discussing a

peace treaty when it came time for a toast. Tension arose over who should drink first when a beautiful serving girl named Coctel (or X'ochitl) grabbed the cup and drained it, solving the impasse, and earning the respect of the American soldiers, who named the drink after her. Whether her name would have been immortalized if she were an *ugly* serving girl is up for question.

8. Cock-ale (see page 200) was a mixed drink made of beer and boiled chicken. It was consumed by eighteenth-century English cock-fighting crowds and was also fed to the cocks themselves to get their strength up, thus transforming them into cannibal fighting cocks.

9. Doctors would sometimes use a cock's tail feather to swab the back of a patient's throat with medicine. Patients with a penchant for partying started gargling the alcohol-based medicine straight, referring to it as "cock's tail."

10. A *kaktel* is a scorpion (whose tail packs a wallop) in the Krio language of Sierra Leone. Although how this would have made it to America, I have no idea.

11. When hosting parties, a nineteenth-century New Orleans apothecary named Peychaud (creator of Peychaud bitters) served mixed drinks in an egg cup known in French as a *coquetier*, which his American friends bastardized into "cocktail."

THERE WAS A YOUNG LADY OF KENT
WHO SAID THAT SHE KNEW WHAT IT MEANT
WHEN MEN ASKED HER TO DINE,
GAVE HER COCKTAILS AND WINE,
SHE KNEW WHAT IT MEANT—BUT SHE WENT!
—ANONYMOUS

Dean Martin

(1917–1995)

Sinatra may have been the Chairman of the Board, but Dean Martin was the one who put the real ring-a-ding in the Rat Pack. Sinatra was a wannabe mobster, a skinny mama's boy from New Jersey who enjoyed threatening the welfare of people's kneecaps. Dean never mouthed off because he didn't have to. He had grown up the real thing.

The son of an Italian immigrant barber, he was born Dino Paul Crocetti. He dropped out of high school to work in a steel mill while pursuing a career as a welterweight boxer under the name "Kid Crochet." But in his hometown of Steubenville, Ohio, there was a more attractive life available.

Steubenville was a mob town. Dino began running booze during Prohibition, and was soon bumped up to card dealer, croupier, and bookie in the gambling joints. This landed him enough mob connections to get singing gigs in nightclubs across the Midwest under the cocktail-crooner name Dean Martini. Show-biz folk encouraged him to lose the Italian connection, and so a nose job and a name job later he became Dean Martin.

He was a minor hit until he teamed up

with Jerry Lewis and became a star as an entertainer.

But when he teamed up with Frank and Sammy Davis Jr., he became a legend as a drunk.

It was the America of JFK, postwar and prosperous. On the Vegas Strip, the crowds packed into the nightclub of the Sands Hotel to see the Rat Pack act out the decadent lifestyle they dreamed of. And slurring his way around the stage with a drink and a cigarette permanently attached to his hand, Dean was the embodiment of a swinging, drinking, cocktail-cool that seemed superhuman.

It was. Dean was actually drinking apple juice onstage and affecting the drunken slur. Not that the persona was a sham, the Rat Pack just saved their legendary carousing for the high-roller suites after the show.

After the assassination of JFK and with the escalation of the Vietnam War, the Rat Pack's lifestyle fell out of favor, but somehow Dean's act still worked. He kept pumping out hit songs and TV celebrity roasts with the same laconic attitude. He became the nation's drunken uncle, who shows up at the Christmas party and makes a fool out of himself, but at the same time, you had to admit that he was damn entertaining as well.

"I feel sorry for people who don't drink. When they wake up in the morning, that's as good as they're going to feel all day."

"You're not drunk if you can lie on the floor without holding on."

"If you drink, don't drive. Don't even putt."

"I've stopped drinking. Now I just freeze it on a stick and eat it like a Popsicle."

"Stay drunk!" —ON HOW TO AVOID A HANGOVER

"The whole world is drunk and we're just the cocktail of the moment. Someday soon, the world will wake up, down two aspirins with a glass of tomato juice, and wonder what the hell all the fuss was about."
—RAT PACK EXISTENTIALISM

FORTIFIED WINES

WINE GONE WILD

PORT

"Port is not for the very young, the vain and the active. It is the comfort of age and the companion of the scholar and the philosopher." —EVELYN WAUGH

Necessity is the mother of invention, and more than most nations, Britain, historically, has needed a drink. The only problem is that its chief source of wine was France, and over the centuries, England and France have had trouble with their dispute-resolution skills. For instance, they kept trying to kill each other.

In 1674, during one of their many skirmishes, the UK banned the import of French wine completely. This sent British shippers scrambling. They went to Portugal and found the town of Oporto (where port wine derives its name).

Far upriver from Oporto is the seventy-mile-long Douro Valley, the harshest wine country in the world. Even today, some of it is only accessible by canoe and donkey. The mountains are so steep and the ground so rocky that wine cultivation wasn't even possible until the Portuguese, with a will to wine that you have to admire, imported soil, dynamited terraces, and even chipped rock by hand to form arable ground.

This sort of climate requires strange grapevines, capable of growing roots twenty-five to sixty-five feet down before they find water. For this reason, the five main grapes used in port are indigenous and are rarely heard of outside Portugal.

The Portuguese still adhere to the old ways—harvesting the grapes by hand in the 100-degree summers, and, to this day, the best grapes are still crushed by foot. Musicians are even brought into the wineries to help the grape stomping pass a little more merrily. The high temperatures fermented the grapes quickly, creating a wine so dark and sharp that the British called it "blackstrap."

The barrels were then rafted down the Douro River (literally, River of Gold) to Oporto, where the British stumbled across it. But how to ship it back to England? During the long voyage, dry wines turned to vinegar and sweet wines actually caused barrels to explode (for an explanation of this, see the chapter on champagne). Somewhere along the line, someone figured out that the higher the alcohol content was, the more stable the wine became. So shippers added brandy. Port was born.

Not only did the higher alcohol content (about 20 percent) make the wine more durable, it also turned it into what Charles Dickens described as "liquid gout," a much stronger and sweeter wine that appealed to the British palate. By the late 1700s, the UK alone imported 36 million bottles.

USELESS AND USEFUL INFORMATION

"Three-Bottle Men"

Port was so popular amongst English aristocrats in the eighteenth century that drinking it became a sort of sport. They acquired the nickname "three-bottle men," because the ability to put away three bottles of port at one sitting became a mark of good breeding, like hunting, riding, or hemophilia.

Born with a Silver Spoon and a Stocked Cellar

A custom started among the upper-crust Brits to celebrate a birth: friends of the family would give the newborn a pipe (about sixty-one cases) of port from his or her birth-year. It would be stored in the cellars, and by the time the child was old enough to drink it, the port would have aged enough to be drunk.

Into Thin Air

Port, like sherry, has to age in barrels for so long it falls victim to evaporation. Every year, port makers lose fifteen thousand bottles to evaporation.

Sorts of Port

There are ten different types of port, but they fall into two basic groups: wood-aged and bottle-aged.

- Tawny is the most popular wood-aged port. It's kept in barrels anywhere from ten to forty years, which lends it a brownish color. The Portuguese drink it with ice during the summer.

■ Vintage is the best bottle-aged port. It's aged in barrels for two years, but requires another couple decades of bottle-aging to mature. Serve at just below room temp., around 65°F (18°C).

SHERRY

"It has a kind of decorum about it. Very proper old ladies can get quietly potted. And clergymen. Won't you have a drink, Reverend? Oh, just a spot of Sherry for me. . . ." —SUMNER LOCKE ELLIOTT

Alcohol makes us do strange things. If a loaf of bread develops mold, we throw it out. But if mold grows on wine, we hail it as a miracle, consecrate a region of Spain for it, and develop painstaking methods to preserve the mold. Such is the case with sherry.

The region is Jerez. The mold is flora. And the sherry is not *just* the sickly sweet old-lady's drink. Sherry comes in two main categories—oloroso is sweet, but fino is a light, dry wine that gained sherry its reputation in a previous century as one of the best wines in the world.

Sherry is as close as British merchants could come to pronouncing the word Jerez, one of the three towns that form the triangular sherry-producing region at the southern tip of Spain. Regular wine arrived there in 1100 B.C., with the Phoenicians, but like an American college girl doing a semester abroad, it developed a whole new personality after being exposed to Spain's unique environment: the soil is a blindingly white limestone made from fossilized shells, and the air is full of a strange yeast known as flora.

Unlike normal wine, which is kept in cellars to protect it from air, sherry *needs* the air for its flavor. After the grapes are turned into wine and spiked with brandy (for the same basic reasons as port), they are put in open barrels. Early Jerez wine makers noticed that when a barrel was left open, the wine quickly became "sick." A yellowish-white foam covered its entire surface. But they also noticed that the flavors the foam gave the wine weren't half-bad. In fact, the longer the flora stuck around, the better the flavor. The problem is yeast feeds on sugar, and when the sugar in a barrel was finished, so was the flora. So the Spaniards created the *solera.*

"IF PENICILLIN CAN CURE THOSE THAT ARE ILL, SPANISH SHERRY CAN BRING THE DEAD BACK TO LIFE."
—SIR ALEXANDER FLEMING

Solera means floor, and refers to where the wine is taken from. Sherry barrels are stacked like a pyramid. The oldest wine, ready to be bottled, is on the bottom row, and when the barrels are partially tapped, they're replenished from the row above, and so on, with the top row being the newest grapes. This ensures fresh sugar in each row, which keeps the flora alive and flavoring (the flora is usually maintained for around six years).

This complicated process was only perfected in the 1800s, but sherry had already gained international attention by the fifteenth century, when the British established trading colonies in Spain and began a minor flirtation with the drink they originally called "sack" (from the French word for dry, *sec*).

But kings will be kings, and after a few sea skirmishes, the king of Spain kicked out the English traders. In 1587, Sir Francis Drake retaliated by attacking Cádiz, where he "singed the King of Spain's beard" and managed to liberate about 420,000 gallons of sherry.

This victory haul proved enough to kick-start a nation of sherry enthusiasts. But because of its pre-*solera* inconsistencies in flavor, sack became the Flaming Moe of the seventeenth century. Like Homer Simpson's concoction, it was a wildly popular drink that was only enjoyed after it was burned first (often by sticking a tankard into the embers of a fire).

Spain and Britain eventually patched things up, and ships of sherry began crisscrossing the ocean, but that created a new problem. As these ships opened up trade with the New World, these countries started producing sherry of their own, of wildly lower quality.

Oddly enough, flora can't exist anywhere except the Jerez region. Foreign wine makers have tried importing the yeast only to watch it die, thus ensuring that sherry is unique to its origins. But that didn't stop other countries from stealing the name. Declining quality resulted in declining sales. Then, teetotaling Victorian England turned against sherry consumption, pushing it even further out of favor, where it remains today, usually only associated with the cooking sherry enjoyed by winos and bored housewives.

The result being that even the best sherry is very reasonably priced, which is why current wine experts go wild over it, rating sherry as one of the best values on the market today.

USELESS AND USEFUL INFORMATION

Better Bookkeeping

Sherry was so popular in seventeenth-century England (as a working wage and a form of entertainment) that bottles and cases of it were used as units in accounting.

AWOL in Andalucía

In 1625, Charles I sent a force of troops to Andalucía to retake British trading posts. They didn't get very far. You see, sherry is stored aboveground to breathe the air (unlike wine in cellars). These huge storage buildings are known as *bodegas*, but locals refer to them as "cathedrals" because of the high-vaulting roofs required for the pyramid-stacked barrels.

The British troops stumbled across a *bodega* and definitely saw it as a sign from God to have a drink. Then another. They never left. The "invasion" only ended several days later when last call was administered by Spanish troops.

Wild Horses

While fighting to retake Spain from the Moors in the thirteenth century, Christian soldiers would feed sherry to their horses before battle to enable them to charge the enemy without fear.

Decades in One Drink

Sherry has no vintage. There can be anywhere from five to fourteen levels in the *solera,* meaning that decades' worth of wine are mixed together in every bottle.

Sherry Stylings

Sherry has twelve different substyles, but those fall into two main categories:

- **Fino:** about 15 percent alcohol. Tends to be pale, light, and dry with an almondy, marzipan-like flavor typified by the Manzanilla style. Serve chilled.

- **Oloroso:** 18–24 percent alcohol. Dark and heavy, with a walnutty flavor. There are some dry styles, but olorosos are mainly sweet, like cream sherry. Serve room temp.

MADEIRA

"A bottle that has long been excluded from the light of day, and is hoary with dust and cobwebs, has been brought into the sunshine; and the golden wine within it sheds a lustre on the table. It is . . . the old Madeira." —CHARLES DICKENS, *DOMBEY AND SON*

Four hundred miles off the coast of Morocco, the volcanic island of Madeira is renowned for two things—its fortified wine and the fact that it's the only place ever discovered by someone named—and this is true—Zarco the Cross-Eyed. Madeira's popularity has waned in the last century, but it's built to see fads come and go.

It is the indestructible wine. Open bottles can last years, and corked bottles can last centuries without losing flavor. The reason is that, along with being spiked with brandy, the wine is literally baked.

In the seventeenth century, trading ships used to store barrels of Madeira wine in their holds as ballast. But as the ships crisscrossed the Equator to the West Indies, the wine would cook in the tropical heat, after which ship captains starting noticing an improvement in its flavor. Madeira makers started sending all their wine on tropical round-trips before bottling it. This only ended in the 1900s, when someone used common sense and realized they could just cook the wine in a vat and save the price of a cruise.

Because of this wanderlust, Madeira became the first wine brought into the United States, and it was the drink used to toast the signing of the Declaration of Independence in 1776.

COCA-WINE

You may have noticed that port, sherry, and Madeira were all fortified with brandy. But why stop with brandy? Why not spike wine with something more interesting like, say, cocaine?

So thought a Corsican man named Angelo Mariani, who in 1863 steeped coca leaves in Bordeaux and created Vin Mariani. Advertisements declared it "unequaled as a tonic-stimulant for fatigued and over-weak body and brain."

Vin Mariani became wildly successful, and was enjoyed by everyone from actors, singers, and writers (H. G. Wells, Jules Verne, Ibsen, Dumas, Zola), to heads of state (presidents Grant and McKinley, Queen Victoria, the czar of Russia), to Thomas Edison and even the pope.

In fact, Pope Leo XIII was so tonic-stimulated that he gave his official endorsement to the drink for an ad campaign. He then awarded Mr. Mariani a special Vatican medal, with a personal note explaining that he "had been supported in his ascetic retirement by a flask of wine which was never empty."

Sales were so good that an American named John Pemberton decided to market a coca-wine of his own. Unfortunately, he lived in Atlanta, which ratified Prohibition in 1886. Forced to ditch the alcohol in his drink, Pemberton substituted coca-wine with coca-sugar water. And that's how Coca-Cola was born.

LIQUEUR

THE MANY REFLECTIONS IN
THE WATERS OF LIFE

Liqueurs, those back-shelf bottles normally reserved for fancy cocktails and aromatic dessert drinks, range from the simplest to some of the most complicated alcohols in the world. The word "liqueur" comes from the Latin word *liquefacere,* which means "to melt, or dissolve." Thus, liqueur is the drink that will melt your face.

All right, not exactly. It's referring to something a twelfth-century French alchemist discovered, which is that during distillation, you can basically dissolve anything into a drink. These potions were thought to be cure-alls, "water of life," that was a gift from God. Or as one French recipe book put it:

> *"This water . . . assuageth the pains and wringings of the belly, killeth worms, and maketh fat folk to become leane. . . ."*

Anxious to killeth worms in the name of God, alchemists and monks took up the call, distilling everything but the kitchen sink: roots, bark, berries, leaves, whatever.

Of course, it was soon realized that liqueurs couldn't cure humans, but at the very least, they could

cure meat. The alcohol helped preserve unrefriger-
ated meat and the aroma disguised the smell if the
meat went rotten. And in a bit of circular logic, anything that could pickle meat could also pickle humans. The Italians in the fourteenth century were the
first to create liqueurs for pleasure.

When Catherine de Médicis married Henry II and
moved into the French court, she brought the party
with her. Soon, every French aristocrat had a small still
brewing their own secret recipe, the more complicated the better.

Recipes grew so complex that they took intense effort, time, and solitude to create. Which is why monasteries perfected many of the most famous liqueurs,
and still manufacture them today. Below are the stories behind a few of these drinks.

Amaretto

In 1525, a young disciple of Leonardo da Vinci was
commissioned to paint a church fresco in Saronno. To
paint the Madonna, he asked the proprietress of the
inn where he was staying to model for him. She did so
gladly, and wanted to thank him for the honor, but she
had no money. So she gathered the apricot pits in the
orchard behind her inn and brewed them with some
herbs. She gave him the resulting drink, and they com-
menced a torrid love affair. The family handed down
her recipe for generations until it was bottled as
amaretto.

Angostura

Created in 1824 by a German doctor sympathetic to
the struggle for Venezuelan independence. He created it as a stomach tonic for Simon Bolívar's troops
fighting in the jungle.

Benedictine

The oldest liqueur, around 1520. The Benedictine monastery was adjacent to swampy marshlands, and the liqueur was originally intended as a cure for malaria.

Drambuie

Gaelic for "golden drink," or "the drink that satisfies." Said to be the personal recipe of Bonnie Prince Charles. He presented it as a token of appreciation to the family who sheltered him on the island of Skye following the collapse of the Scottish clans' rebellion of 1745.

Campari

Created in 1860 by a café owner named Gaspare Campari to serve to his patrons in celebration of Italy's unification that year. It later became wildly popular in the United States during Prohibition, when it wasn't considered an alcohol. It was a digestive bitter . . . that just happened to be 48 proof.

Tia Maria

This rum-based coffee liqueur was the recipe of a wealthy Spanish family living in Jamaica in the seventeenth century. As the brutal fighting of the colonial wars drew near, the family was forced to flee their home and they got separated from their daughter. A loyal maidservant managed to rescue her and recover the family jewelry box, which contained a pair of black pearl earrings and the most treasured family heirloom—the recipe for the drink that the family then named in the maid's honor, Tia Maria (Aunty Mary).

SAKE

PROSPEROUS WATERS
OF THE RISING SUN

"Moonlight steeped in spring rain,
Blossoms of wisdom—
All from one little cup."
—LI PO, CHINESE POET

Alongside samurai, sushi, and strange animation, sake has a central role in the iconography of Japan. But for wannabe buffs, sake is a beginner's nightmare. It has just as many complexities and permutations as wine, but without the Roman alphabet on the label to help us out. So it ends up seeming a little like Japan itself, fascinating but slightly impenetrable.

Oddly enough, for a drink that's so identified with Japanese culture, sake's origins actually lie in China, probably around 4800 B.C. To make rice wine, the Japanese first needed rice, and rice cultivation didn't make it over from the mainland until 200 B.C. And wherever rice traveled, rice wine wasn't far behind.

It quickly became known as "The Drink of the Gods," and was woven into Japanese mythology (drunken eight-headed dragons and so on, see "Matsuo-sama," page 190) and religious practices. It was specially brewed by monks for use in Shinto fertility and harvest festivals. The word "sake" itself is derived from *saké-mizu*, which means "prosperous waters."

But back then, its full name was *kuchikami no saké*, or "chewed-in-the-mouth sake," because the whole village would gather and grind the rice into a mash by chewing it and then spitting it into a tub. The enzymes in the spit would break the starches down into sugar so fermentation could begin.

Of course, even in small villages, you never know where everybody's mouth has been, so many villages allowed only the young female virgins to chew the rice. Virgins were considered to be mediums to the gods, and so they produced *bijinshu*, or "beautiful woman sake." In some rural areas of Japan, this practice only ended a few decades ago.

But salivating virgins soon became more of an aesthetic choice after an alternative was discovered— mold. Rice mold, to be exact. *Koji*, as it's known, performs the same enzyme functions as saliva. Plus, with the introduction of grinding wheels to polish the rice, it no longer took a village to make sake. It could be done by individuals.

And anything good enough to be "The Drink of the Gods" wasn't going to stay sacred for long. Sake officially went secular in A.D. 689, when the Imperial Court created its own Imperial Sake Department. In the cities, sake became the drink of the upper classes, but in the countryside, every rice farmer had his own still.

"Get drunk before colorful flowers in order to absorb their light and color; at night get drunk in the snow to clear your thoughts."—RULES FOR GETTING DRUNK WITH ELEGANCE AND DIGNITY BY LIU LING, ONE OF THE SEVEN WISE MEN OF THE BAMBOO GROTTO (NOT THAT I KNOW WHAT THE BAMBOO GROTTO IS, BUT IT SOUNDS REALLY COOL), A.D. SIXTH CENTURY

In the 1300s, Japan went through an industrial revolution, and large-scale production became possible. Some upper-class merchants decided to start breweries, but they didn't know how to make the stuff, they just drank it. So who better to hire than the moonshining farmers who'd been brewing their own hooch all along?

"WITHOUT FLOWING WINE
WHAT GOOD TO ME ARE LOVELY
CHERRY TREES IN BLOOM?"
—ANONYMOUS SEVENTEENTH-CENTURY HAIKU

It was the perfect relationship. Once the harvest was over, farmers had nothing to do during winter. So they followed their rice crops into the city breweries, leaving their farms and families behind to band together into a clan led by the *toji* (master brewer). Based on the quality of local water and the *toji*'s skill, each province developed its own style and secret recipe, which was jealously guarded from competing clans. The tradition of sake as a farmer's art lasted up until only a few decades ago (scientists have now replaced them).

But something interesting happened. The sake merchants became very rich. And, suddenly, sake was a source of taxable income (which meant wealth and, more importantly, power) for the feudal shoguns. The shoguns embraced and encouraged the breweries.

Not only was sake inextricably woven into the religious and secular aspects of Japanese culture, it was now sponsored by and sponsoring the government. This concept has held true even up into modern times. In 1904, the Ministry of Finance created an official Sake Research Center to help improve and refine sake brewing, because better sake = bigger drinking = bigger tax revenues.

Sacred, secular, and state—sake hit the cultural trifecta.

Sadly, sake's status has been in steady decline ever since Japan opened up to the West. As of a couple of years ago, Japan had about eighteen hundred sake breweries, producing as many as ten thousand different types of sakes. But that number goes down every year. Beer now accounts for over three-quarters of alcohol consumption in Japan.

On the plus side, sake sales have grown exponentially in the West as people make the same discovery as Marco Polo did during his travels, that "being very hot stuff, it makes one drunk sooner than any other wine."

USELESS AND USEFUL INFORMATION

The Sake Experience

There's a real zen of sake, and the Japanese have phrases describing the charms of each different drinking session. Two of the best are:

- *Tsukimi-Zaké:* Drinking sake while watching a full moon.

- *Yukimi-Zaké:* Drinking sake while watching the snow fall.

Jump In, the Sake's Fine

A *sakaburo* is a hot bath with one-half liter to a liter of sake added to the water. This is said to be good for circulation and the skin. Some fancy cosmetic lines use sake as the secret ingredient in their bath products.

Brand-Name Haiku

Sake labels tend to have very poetic names. Some of the best are: Demon-slayer, Man Mountain, Mist of the Harbor, Courage of the Warrior, Chrysanthemum Princess, Drunken Whale, 7 Gods of Good Fortune, Hiroshima University Stories.

Infinite Flavors

There are reputed to be four hundred flavor components in sake. In comparison, wine has only two hundred. This means that either sake is more complicated than wine, or the Japanese are better at being fussy about their drinks. You make the call.

They Like 'Em Young

Sake doesn't age well. Avoid any bottle that's over a year old. It's best within the first six to seven months, and should be stored in a cool place away from light.

Dueling Proverbs

There is a Japanese saying: "You know good sake the next morning." Premium sake is so pure it's reputedly hangover free. But test at your own risk, since there's another Japanese saying: "Sake starts out as a friend but can end as an enemy."

ABSINTHE

"Absinthe makes the tart grow fonder."
—ERNEST DOWSON, BRITISH POET

Absinthe, much fabled for its reputed hallucinogenic qualities, is a 60 to 70 percent liquor related to gin and distilled from the wormwood plant. Wormwood itself has been used in alcohol for thousands of years: the ancient Greeks soaked its leaves in their wine to remedy various illnesses.

But absinthe as we know it started in 1792, when a French physician named Dr. Pierre Ordinaire (literally: Dr. Ordinary) fled the French Revolution and settled in Couvet, Switzerland. Locals had already been distilling wormwood, which grew wild in the region, but it was Ordinaire who bottled and promoted it as a medicinal cure-all. This was a bold claim considering its side effects include convulsions, hallucinations, blindness, loss of hearing, mania, stupor, death, and, even worse, gastrointestinal irritation.

Despite these drawbacks, and its infamously terrible taste, absinthe became the rage of all Europe in the second half of the nineteenth century. It was during this era that the drink acquired its mythic status (and

associations with the wild Moulin Rouge days of Paris)
after being championed by such writers as Byron,
Wilde, and Baudelaire, and artists like Manet, Degas,
and Toulouse-Lautrec.

> "HE SAW HIS GLASS OF ABSINTHE GROW
> AND GROW UNTIL HE FELT HIMSELF IN THE
> CENTER OF ITS OPAL LIGHT, WEIGHTLESS,
> COMPLETELY DISSOLVED IN THIS STRANGE
> ATMOSPHERE." —RAINER MARIA RILKE, POET

However, in 1905, the party came to a crashing
halt. A Swiss laborer named Jean Lanfray, after a full
day of drinking, got into a fight with his pregnant wife
over who should milk the family cow, upon which Mrs.
Lanfray accused her husband of laziness. This was a
fair point, as her husband was known to consume six
quarts of wine, six brandies, and two absinthes *every
day*. Still, he took exception to such name-calling, and
ended the argument by shooting her, and then their
two daughters (ages four and a half and two), before
botching his own suicide attempt.

Lanfray had consumed his normal range of spirits
that day, but taking their cue from his final premurder
aperitif, the papers immediately dubbed this the "Absinthe Murders." This might not have been so bad, except that a few days later, another man in an
absinthe-fueled rage hacked his wife to death with a
hatchet. From a marketing point of view, this was not
helpful. Although it must be said that in terms of PR, it
only added to the legend.

Stemming from these murders, and the growing
recognition of its health hazards, absinthe was soon
banned in most major countries. In recent years, however, it is starting to reappear across Europe.

MISCELLANIEST

- The much-maligned Jell-O shot has a finer pedigree than most frat parties would lead you to suppose. At upper-class parties in the mid-1800s, punches were chilled into a jelly and served in slices on hot summer evenings. Several recipes were included in *The Bon Vivant's Companion*, the first cocktail book, published in 1862. The book cautions, however, that "many persons have been tempted to partake so plentifully of it as to render them somewhat unfit for waltzing or quadrilling after supper."

- In Mexico, there was a drink known as *potación de guaya*, or "drink of grief," which was wine or brandy in which marijuana buds were steeped. When referring to marijuana in America, the *potación* part got shortened, which is where we get the slang term "pot."

- China produces a Three Penis wine, which is said to cure anemia, shingles, and memory loss, plus act as an aphrodisiac. The penises in question are from a seal, a dog, and a deer. They are described as "robust and nutritious."

- The Uape Indians of the Upper Amazon in Brazil mix the ashes of their cremated dead into *casiri,* their alcoholic beverage. To honor the deceased, the members of the family—young and old alike—then drink it. The Cocomba tribe of Peru has the same tradition. They believe that the dead are better off staying warm inside a family member than in the cold, cold ground.

- In the jungles of Central and South America, some Indian tribes make *chichi,* an alcoholic drink made from available grains and their own spit. (Why spit? Read "Sake," page 177.)

- In China, many of the local beers forgo traditional preservatives in favor of formaldehyde. Apparently, this gives the beer extra zing. Unfortunately, it also gives you cancer.

- In Vietnam, the small town of Le Mat is also known as Snake Village. For a thousand years, locals have been making drinks like snake-fetus wine, snake-bile wine, and, for that modern touch, lizard wine with Diet Coke. You can also witness a live snake's heart cut out and served—still beating—in a shot glass of snake-blood wine. Besides curing a variety of aches and pains, it's rumored to be the Viagra of Vietnam.

Amateur Food and Drink Matching Guide

"Red wine with fish. Well, that should have told me something." —James Bond, upon discovering his dinner host is a double agent, *From Russia with Love*

There are hundreds of extremely long-winded books on pairing food and drinks, but here are some generally agreed-upon recommendations. An asterisk (*) indicates pairings that are considered time-honored classics.

Beer

Cheese—bitter or Belgian Trappist Beer.*
Red meat/steak—ale.
Barbecued meats—India pale ale or stout.
Pork or chicken—malty lager.
Sausages—dark lager or Oktoberfest beers.*
Oysters—Guinness.*
Fish—golden lager or pilsner.
Mussels—Belgian lambic.*
Fried foods—wheat beer.

Wine

Steak—Cabernet Sauvignon or Zinfandel.
Roast beef—Pinot Noir or Merlot.
Roast chicken—Chianti.
Lamb—Cabernet or Rioja.
Plain fish—Chenin Blanc.
Salmon—Sauvignon Blanc.
Pizza—Merlot or Rioja.
Pasta—

> *with tomato sauce*—Chianti or Sangiovese red.
> *with Bolognese sauce*—Cabernet Sauvignon.
> *with cream sauce*—Pinot Grigio.

Champagne

Grilled seafood or vegetables, sushi, raw oysters, strawberries and cream,* pizza (it helps cut the grease).

Rum

The classic pairing with rum is citrus fruit, and a popular eighteenth-century dessert was orange slices soaked in rum. Also pork, chocolate, and cigars (to smoke, not eat).

Whiskey

Seafood, steak, cigars.
Smoked meats and cheeses, game—Scotch.
Barbecued/grilled meat—bourbon.

Tequila

Spicy food with chili peppers,* pork, flan, seafood, citrus fruits.

Vodka

Pickles, caviar,* sausages, salted or pickled fish on rye bread,* black bread.

Gin

Red meat.

Brandy

Nut and apple desserts.
Duck—cognac.*

Port

Walnuts or almonds (plain or in cake or tarts).*

Sherry

Olives,* shellfish,* smoked salmon—dry
   sherry (fino or Manzanilla).
**Soft, mature cheese (blue cheese,
   especially*)**—sweet or cream sherry.

Sake

Sushi,* tempura, white meats like chicken and pork. No red meat.

GOD AND THE BOTTLE

"Bacchus, n. A convenient deity invented by the ancients as an excuse for getting drunk."
—**AMBROSE BIERCE**

If you were to sum up the entire history of alcohol and its impact on civilization from its prehistoric origins to modern times, you could do it in three words: God, masses, taxes.

Unfortunately, my publisher wouldn't pay me for just writing out those three words, so this book has to be a bit more expansive on each of those subjects. The first, God, is how mankind first regarded alcohol, as a sacred gift to be used in religious ceremonies. The second is when alcohol becomes secularized, when the masses figure out that this drink the priests reserve for special occasions actually tastes good, helps relax you after a day of work, and goes great with sporting events. Finally, alcohol is instituted as one of the basic structures of our society when nations support themselves by placing a tax on our habit.

But it's the first one, the sacred, which is probably the most interesting, because it speaks to our relationship with the world we found ourselves in the day we stopped being monkeys and started being humans. The worship of a god and the ingestion of alcohol both served as ways for early man to lift himself out of his earthbound, often wretched conditions, if only for a few fleeting moments. It's no wonder that the two became intertwined.

Some religions incorporate alcohol into the very foundation of their beliefs. Some reject it outright. But whether for it or against it, every religion addresses the concept of alcohol.

> "A BARREL OF WINE CAN WORK MORE MIRA-
> CLES THAN A CHURCH FULL OF SAINTS."
>
> —ITALIAN PROVERB

LORDS OF THE DRINK

Dionysus/Bacchus

The Greek/Roman god of wine. The name "Bacchus" translates as "the god who is worshipped with loud cries." And modern names like Dennis and Denise are derived from Dionysus. The wine-god mythology was so popular in early culture that other religions had a hard time competing. So early Christians tried a little counterprogramming—they declared December 25 to be the day Jesus was born because that was the same day people celebrated the birth of Dionysus (for more on the Dionysus/Christ connection, see "The Blood and the Body," page 37).

Matsuo-sama

The patron deity of sake making. Sake plays a central role in Shinto religious festivals, where it's offered to the gods in thanks for successful harvests, weddings, New Years, etc. But sake is also a means of actually contacting the gods. In the *O-miki* ritual, the priest drinks sake to imbue himself with the god-force. In this state, he can communicate with the deities and ask them for blessings of good luck.

According to Japan's oldest chronicle, the *Kojiki*, sake dates back to the mythological "age of the gods." In this story, the princess Kushinada is kidnapped by the Great Serpent of Yamata Lake, an eight-headed dragon with eight tails that stretched over eight valleys and eight hills. The sun goddess's brother, Susanoonomikoto (Susan, to his friends), saves her by brewing eight vats of sake for the dragon, one per head. When the dragon becomes intoxicated, Susan cuts off its heads and its tails and in the last tail, he finds a special sword. This sword became one of the three symbols that represent the Shinto religion and the coat of arms of the imperial family.

"THE SAGE CONFUCIUS SAID
THE DRINKING OF SAKE KNOWS NO BOUNDS—
HE MUST HAVE BEEN A VERY GOOD DRINKER.
THE LORD BUDDHA ADMONISHED THAT
DRINKING INVOLVES THIRTY-SIX EVILS—
HE MUST HAVE BEEN A VERY POOR DRINKER."

—NINETEENTH-CENTURY SONG LYRICS
BY KIKUOKA OF KYOTO

Tepoztecal

Aztec god of alcoholic merriment. But he plays a distant second fiddle to Mayahuel, the goddess of fertility, who's responsible for giving mankind the agave plant (which tequila and its precursor, pulque, are made from). Her husband then hurled lightning at the agave plant, which magically transformed the thunderbolt into a fermented sap that came oozing out. After sampling this fermented lightning, the Aztecs named the plant *metl* in her honor, which is where we derived the word "mescal."

A racier legend claims that Mayahuel fell in love with an Aztec warrior and produced an alcoholic elixir from her breast for him to drink. The Aztecs seemed pretty obsessed with their goddess's breasts, because Mayahuel had four hundred of them that she used to feed her four hundred rabbit-children, each of whom represented a different form of intoxication.

The Aztecs rated their drunkenness on a sliding scale of rabbits. So two rabbits was a slight buzz and four hundred rabbits meant you were about to communicate with the gods. Despite this, only priests were ever allowed to drink more than four glasses of pulque at a time. They did this in order to communicate with the gods, and also to psyche them up for the human sacrifice and possible cannibalism involved in their rituals. But in a nice tip of the hat to old folks, seniors were exempt from all these drinking laws.

Ogoun

A Haitian voodoo warrior spirit who possesses people in order to give them power and dominance. Those possessed by Ogoun will wash their hands in flaming rum and feel no pain. Ogoun loves to drink and when he occupies a human, they will demand rum from others with the phrase *"Gren mwe fret"* ("My testicles are cold").

(*Author's note:* If there's one dream I hold for this book, it's that everyone who reads it will begin asking for drinks from friends or bartenders with the phrase "My testicles are cold." How great would that be? Seriously?)

Rum is used to summon a great number of spirits in the voodoo religion, and for good reason. Rum and voodoo are both abused children born from the slave trade. When Africans were shipped to the cane fields of the Caribbean to make rum, they brought their various tribal religions with them. Mixed with some missionary-taught Christianity and created under the violent conditions of slavery, voodoo took on a darker, stick-it-to-whitey undercurrent. And rum became the fuel for the religion. Contact with the spirit world is made by drinking large amounts of rum and dancing in a frenzy (to drums carved from trees that have also been fed rum) until a person becomes possessed, and sometimes sexually mounted, by a spirit.

In Jamaica, sugarcane cutters will leave the first few stalks at the beginning of a row uncut. These are then twisted and tied together to resemble a human watchman, who will scare off "duppies," or evil spirits, while they work.

Mbaba Mwana Waresa

Also known as Lady Rainbow. The Zulu goddess of rainbows, agriculture, rain, and beer. She defied the other gods by falling in love with a mortal man. Because of this new love, she wanted to see all mankind happy, so she gave them the gift of beer.

In Greek myth, Pandora opens a box and releases all the evils into the world. But the salvation of mankind, the thing that keeps us from leading lives of despair, is the fact that she closed the lid just in time to keep one thing from escaping—hope. There is an African myth that is very similar, only the source of mankind's salvation in the box isn't "hope," it's a gourd of beer.

> "THERE'S NOUGHT NO DOUBT SO MUCH THE
> SPIRIT CALMS AS RUM AND TRUE RELIGION."
>
> —LORD BYRON

Hathor

The ancient Egyptian goddess of both love and destruction, which is the perfect definition of her other title, "The Mistress of Intoxication." Actually, the Egyptians had a whole host of gods for beer, wine, and drunkenness, but Hathor plays the biggest role in their mythology.

In *The Book of the Heavenly Cow*, the sun god, Ra, sends Hathor down to earth to punish mankind for not showing him enough respect. Hathor turns into a lion and goes on such a rampage that she's soon wading in a sea of human blood, occasionally drinking at it to fuel her frenzy. This goes on for three days and nights and Ra eventually becomes worried that she could wipe out the whole human race. So he adds fruit and barley to the blood and transforms it into the world's first beer. When Hathor takes a sip, she instantly mellows out and decides to give the killing a rest. Mankind is saved.

Heidrun

Heaven's bartender in Viking myth. Heidrun is a mythic goat whose udder provides a never-ending stream of mead for the pleasure of Vikings who were brave enough to earn entrance into the afterworld of Valhalla.

To celebrate the winter solstice in December, the Vikings brewed a special beer to pay tribute to the

Norse gods. But that sort of pagan worship became unacceptable after they converted to Christianity around the eleventh century. So instead, they brewed a special beer to pay tribute to Jesus and the Virgin Mary. This wasn't done lightly, either. Anyone who failed to make a Christmas ale (and drink it) had to pay a fine to the bishop, and was in danger of being kicked out of the village.

Osmator

"The Bride Adviser." A little farther north in Finland, Osmator and two other women were unsuccessful in making beer until they used saliva to start the fermentation. Only, to make the beer more bad-ass, they took the spit directly from the mouth of a bear.

The Finns liked their beer so much that in their creation myth, the *Kalevala*, there are four hundred stanzas devoted to the creation of beer, and only two hundred to the creation of the world.

> "IT IS MY DESIGN TO DIE IN THE BREW-HOUSE; LET ALE BE PLACED TO MY MOUTH WHEN I AM EXPIRING, THAT WHEN THE CHOIRS OF ANGELS COME, THEY MAY SAY, 'BE GOD PROPITIOUS TO THIS DRINKER.'"
> —SAINT COLUMBANUS A.D. 612

Saint Martin of Tours

(A.D. 315–397). The patron saint of grape growers, pub owners, and ramblers. He can be called upon by wine makers to provide the right amounts of sunshine and moisture to ensure a good harvest.

Saint Martin pioneered the concept of a church or monastery planting its own vineyards for sacramental, medicinal, and beverage purposes. Considering how much land the Church owned, this transformed Europe into a wine continent in one fell swoop.

It's his donkey, however, who's given even more credit. The wine of the time couldn't match the quality of the old Roman wine and no one could figure out why. According to legend, Saint Martin's donkey was left tethered to a bush one day and nibbled all the grapevines within reach down to below knee-level. After the monks salvaged what grapes they could from the vines, they were astonished to discover that it produced their best wine ever. The donkey had accidentally replicated the long-lost Roman technique wherein a lower yield produces better-flavored grapes.

Saint Brigid

(A.D. 453–525). Classic quote: "I should like a great lake of beer for the King of Kings, I should like the angels of heaven to be drinking it through time eternal."

Among the miracles counted toward this Irish woman's sainthood are: She once changed her bathwater to beer to offer to a traveling and thirsty clergyman. And on a separate occasion, "when the lepers she nursed implored her for beer, and there was none to be had, she changed the water which was ready for a bath into an excellent beer, by the sheer strength of her blessing, and dealt it out to the thirsty in plenty." In retrospect, it is clear that Saint Brigid had a problem, as hiding alcohol in the bathroom is one of the hallmarks of an alcoholic.

The Catholic Church has always had a fairly relaxed attitude toward drink, considering (a) the blood of Christ is wine and (b) the Church is based in Rome. With its Italian bent, the Church became a major proponent of wine throughout Europe. And as the Church ventured forth into pagan, beer-drinking countries like Germany, it encouraged wine consumption as a way of getting right with God, although it eventually came to embrace beer as well. In fact, the early Church declared that all alcohol was a gift from God to be enjoyed. Abstaining was all right, but actively disliking alcohol was heresy.

> "IF GOD FORBADE DRINKING, WOULD HE HAVE MADE WINE SO GOOD?"
> —CARDINAL RICHELIEU

Pope Urban VII (reigned 1623–1644), surely the funkiest-named pope of all time, encouraged public celebrations by having the fountains of Rome filled with red wine. . . . *But* he wasn't *too* magnanimous. He used it as a ploy to earn money, taxing people who drank.

As for the popes themselves, for hundreds of years, they've been enjoying a specially pressed wine reserved for the personal use of His Holiness and immediate staff. It's made from a centuries-old vine that's cultivated and preserved inside the Vatican itself, thus ensuring that the pope is able to drink wine made from the same grapes as his predecessors.

Nowadays, at the Vatican City grocery store, slower-selling wines are given what's officially called the "Papal Discount," a massive slash in price to help move them off the shelf. Unfortunately, to qualify for the discount, Vatican residence is required.

Church Ale

Also known as Holy Ale. English priests and monks had to pay for the upkeep of their own Church. To raise funds, they would brew a special Church Ale and throw a villagewide party. Some of the Church Ale parties would last for three days, and at one particular shindig in the thirteenth century, free ale was given out to any bachelor who, on the final day, could successfully stand up.

A DRINK A DAY

As you read through this book from a modern perspective, it's hard not to shake your head in wonder at the heroic consumption that took place throughout history: cocktails were a morning drink; babies were fed beer; brandy was prescribed by doctors. But it's not that they were just big ol' drunks (although they were certainly that), they had a good reason for drinking. It's the same reason that vodka, whiskey, Scandinavian aquavit, and French eau-de-vie all translate into the same thing, "water of life."

In modern times, we're all fairly clued in to the concept that a glass of wine a day is good for you, but back then, they weren't thinking about their cholesterol levels and the merits of antioxidants in red wine. No, for them drinking was healthy for the same reason that a nurse rubs your arm with alcohol before jabbing in a needle. Alcohol is a sterilizing agent. It kills bacteria. And in the untreated, sewage-infested water supplies of cities and towns before the twentieth century, there was plenty of bacteria. Drinking beer, wine, or spirits was *far* more hygienic than drinking water.

They didn't know that, of course. This was before

Louis Pasteur introduced the world to the concept of bacteria (a discovery he made while investigating the mysterious process of fermentation for a distiller). Before that, people just sort of noticed that the ones who drank lots of alcohol weren't dropping dead as quickly as the ones who stuck to water. Plus, alcohol made them *feel* good. It's easy to see how putting these two together produced the general folk wisdom that drinking was good for you.

> "IT WAS MY UNCLE GEORGE WHO DISCOVERED THAT ALCOHOL WAS A FOOD WELL IN ADVANCE OF MODERN MEDICAL THOUGHT."
>
> —P. G. WODEHOUSE

Because of this, the medical profession has had a long-term relationship with alcohol (see "Brandy," and "Liqueur"). And even though there was a basis in truth to these beliefs, like most remedies based on folk wisdom, it regularly crossed the line into fantastic quackery.

Doctor's Orders

- One of the first known references to spirits in Europe comes from a fourteenth-century manuscript written by an Italian doctor. His recommendations include mixing brandy with white wine and honey to improve memory, mixing in rosemary and sage as a tincture against worms, and using it in a cold compress to cure ailments of the breasts.

- In seventeenth-century British hospitals, a sick child's weekly food ration included two gallons of beer.

- In the 1800s, rum was considered excellent for cleaning hair and keeping it healthy.

- In the nineteenth century, the Brunonian School of Medicine was introduced. This was a treatment based on the idea that alcohol rebalanced the system. It prescribed up to three pints of brandy a day for virtually any illness. For obvious reasons, it became very popular.

- In the 1880s, Bacardi rum got a big marketing boost when Alfonso XIII, the future king of Spain, came down with grippe. Court doctors included Bacardi rum in the king's recovery regimen, allowing Bacardi to advertise itself as "the rum that saved His Majesty's life."

> "IF YOU RESOLVE TO GIVE UP SMOKING, DRINKING AND LOVING, YOU DON'T ACTUALLY LIVE LONGER, IT JUST SEEMS LONGER."
>
> —CLEMENT FREUD

Health Drinks

PIG RINSE: This combination of champagne and crème de cassis was a popular digestive aid and stomach tonic in turn-of-the-century France. We now know this drink as "kir." The name was changed to honor the mayor of Dijon, a resistance fighter named Canon Felix Kir. The mayor's thoughts about having his name affixed to a drink previously called "pig rinse" are unknown.

COCK-ALE: A seventeenth-century drink prepared by housewives by taking "one large and elderly cockerel," sticking him in a bag and pulverizing his body (old recipe books advise he be "flea-ed first"). Then boil in twelve gallons of beer with four pounds of raisins and some nutmeg until the cock is jelly. Press well, and drink. It's a "restorative drink, which contributes much to the invigorating of nature."

GROANING ALE: Used up until the end of the nineteenth century, this was a strong, dark beer specially brewed for women going through labor. It was used to relax the muscles and ease any pain.

METAL WATER: In 1351, a Belgian alchemist named Johannes van Aalter formulated a fantastic new way to treat skin diseases. The recipe for "water from metals and of great strength" called for iron, lead, tin, copper, silver, and gold shavings to be soaked in seven liquids over seven days according to this strict schedule:

Day 1 . . . urine of a young virgin
Day 2 . . . warm wine
Day 3 . . . juice of a fennel
Day 4 . . . white of an egg
Day 5 . . . milk of a woman who had given birth to a boy and nursed him
Day 6 . . . red wine
Day 7 . . . white of seven eggs

All seven liquids were then distilled together into a concentrated alcoholic substance. But before you race off to acquire some virgin urine, you should know that the recipe is incomplete. It fails to specify whether the final result is an ointment or a beverage.

"OF DOCTORS AND MEDICINES WE HAVE IN PLENTY MORE THAN ENOUGH . . . WHAT YOU MAY, FOR THE LOVE OF GOD, SEND IS SOME LARGE QUANTITY OF BEER."

—DISPATCH FROM THE AUSTRALIAN COLONY, NEW SOUTH WALES, 1854

Surgeon Generals of Yore

London's gin craze inspired the first health warning to appear on a bottle of alcohol in 1751. Mind you, the language was a little more high-minded back then:

> *"When famed Pandora to the clouds withdrew*
> *From her dire box, unnumbered evils flew.*
> *No less a curse this vehicle contains:—*
> *Fire to the mind and poison to the veins."*

A Pint of Beer, a Bowl of Pretzels, and One Corpse, Please

In London in the early 1800s, medical school anatomy classes were only legally allowed to dissect the bodies of convicted murderers. Consequently, a black market sprang up as "sack-'em-up" men began robbing graves to meet the shortage. Pubs near medical schools became places where students could order a pint and a corpse that was hidden in the back.

The slums of Dublin became a big resource for bodies that no one would notice missing. But the bodies had to be shipped cheaply, clandestinely, arrive in fairly good condition, and, if possible, include the requisite Irish screw-you gesture to the English. Irish smugglers solved all these problems at once by shipping the corpses *in barrels of Irish whiskey*!

Spontaneous Human Combustion

During the gin craze in eighteenth-century London, excessive drinking fueled the urban legend of spontaneous human combustion (SHC). The worry was that the build-up of flammable alcohol in the body could reach a point where the slightest spark would set you off like a bottle rocket.

It wasn't only commoners who bought into it. Medical treatises were written. Research was conducted. Of course, such a dramatic death didn't escape the attention of pulp writers, who quickly incorporated it into their fiction. And just to show that the high-falutin' authors we're taught to revere weren't quite as high-falutin' when they were writing, SHC claims a drunken sailor in Herman Melville's *Redburn* (1849). And in *Bleak House* (1852), Charles Dickens dispatches the alcoholic character, Krook, in a scene worthy of Stephen King:

> *"[There was] a smouldering, suffocating vapour in the room and a dark greasy coating on the walls and ceiling."* . . .
>
> *"Here is a small burnt patch of flooring . . . and here is—is it the cinder of a small charred and broken leg of wood sprinkled with white ashes, or is it coal? O Horror, he is here! . . . Spontaneous Combustion."*

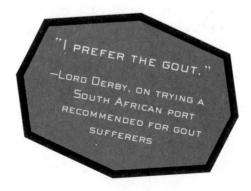

"I PREFER THE GOUT."
—LORD DERBY, ON TRYING A SOUTH AFRICAN PORT RECOMMENDED FOR GOUT SUFFERERS

BRITISH ROYAL NAVY

Before planes, trains, and automobiles, before the Internet and phones, the world was connected and ruled by ships. And the British Royal Navy ruled the waves. With military supremacy came commercial dominance as well. British trading ships controlled the lion's share of the commercial trade, and by dint of good timing, all of this came at a turning point in history.

The British only became the world's uncontested superpower after it pulled the plug on the Spanish Armada in 1588. By that time, the New World, the Far East, and Africa had all been discovered, and trading ships were beginning to tie them together. In effect, the British took charge of the globe during the first spasm of globalization.

It's fair to say that from this position of power, they played a role in the spread of many products (tea, tobacco, spices, etc.). But it's also fair to say that—all stereotypes aside here—historically, the British had a *particular* love for those products that could get them loaded. They played a major role in the history of whiskey, gin, champagne, rum, cider, beer, sherry, and port.

Or, rather, British sailors did. Shipping was the life-line between the empires and their far-flung colonies. Commerce and culture flowed through the port towns, which were influenced by the oceangoing culture of British sailors. Whatever interested *them* is what made it onto their ships (and to other parts of the world) with the greatest care and in the greatest quantity. And what interested sailors was alcohol.

Stuck out at sea in dangerous, rat-infested ships for months at a time with nothing but a bunch of scurvy, unwashed, illiterate men as company and the empty ocean horizon for a view. It's no wonder that after battening down all the hatches and trimming all the sails, there wasn't a hell of a lot for a crew to do but contemplate buggery and the bottle.

An entire culture sprang up around drinking, with a code of conduct and a language all its own, some of which has even worked its way into our everyday English language.

THE OFFICERS

British naval officers—the ultimate artisans of the stiff upper lip. They lived lives wholly separate from their crew. They ate, drank, and socialized away from their unwashed men, and as such developed their own distinct subculture of drinking. The primary aspect being that with higher rank came better drink. When the crew drank beer, officers drank wine and port (about half a gallon a day). And when the crew switched to rum, officers became gin and brandy connoisseurs.

Devil's Toothbrush

An equal mixture of brandy and gin, taken neat by officers after meals. With a boatload of scurvy-prone men, before the advent of toothpaste, this was as close to a cure for morning breath as it got.

Traditional Toasts

Officers at sea followed a strict weekly schedule for toasts when drinking after dinner. (Possible alternatives noted after a semicolon.)

Sunday	Absent friends
Monday	Our ships at sea; Queen and country
Tuesday	Our men, Our mothers; Health and wealth
Wednesday	Ourselves (as no one else is likely to concern themselves with our welfare), Our swords, Old ships (i.e., shipmates)
Thursday	A bloody war or a sickly season (as promotions only came after the death of your superior); The king
Friday	A willing foe and sea room; Fox hunting and old port
Saturday	Sweethearts and wives (may they never meet)

Gin Pennant

The nickname given to the green and white flag that signals an invitation to come aboard, and presumably share refreshments and good cheer with the officers.

THE CREW

Up until the eighteenth century, crewmen received a ration of a gallon of beer a day (that's about eight pints). Apart from the buzz, beer was used as an alternate water supply, since a ship's drinking water stagnated quickly. In fact, the navy had its own brewery in England, which had to produce 4 million gallons a year to meet demand.

But on long voyages, beer would turn putrid as well. So when the British navy went to the Caribbean and discovered the durability of rum, it quickly switched allegiance (see "Sailor's Delight," page 103). The sailors' daily ration or "tot" became half a pint of rum, with half received at lunchtime and the other half at supper (taken from a barrel inscribed with the slogan "God Save the Queen"). But as the civilized world began creeping into the sailors' world, concerns over drunkenness cut the ration in half in 1825, and then in half again in 1850.

By World War I, the ration had become so insignificant that in several instances, British sailors traded large deck guns from their ships to U.S. sailors for a bottle of Scotch. And submarine sailors took to "torpedo juice," the pure grain alcohol used to fuel the torpedo's motor, which they would water down and flavor with canned fruit.

Finally, on what became known as "Black Tot Day," July 31, 1970, the British navy did away with its alcohol ration altogether. British ships all over the world gave their kegs an official burial at sea, wrapped in Union Jack flags and with pipers playing in a minor key.

Nelson's Aftertaste

Lord Nelson, the admiral who defeated Napoleon's navy, was killed during the Battle of Trafalgar (1805). Most sailors are buried at sea, but as an admiral he had to be brought back to land for an official burial. To preserve his body during the voyage, the commander of the ship stored Nelson's body in the vat of rum and halted all rum rations to the crew.

When the ship reached port, officials went to retrieve Nelson's body and found the vat was bone-dry. The crew had been secretly tapping and drinking it the whole way home. After that, naval rum was referred to as "Nelson's Blood."

Proof

The concept of "proof" started in the British naval yards of Jamaica. The percentage of alcohol in a spirit was measured with a simple test—it was poured over a small amount of gunpowder and lit on fire. If the rum's percentage wasn't high enough, the flame would fizzle out. If it was, a blue flame would burn and the gunpowder would explode. This was very literally "proof" of the rum's strength. To explode, it had to be 50 percent alcohol, or 100 proof. As to why a drink being strong enough to blow up gunpowder was considered just the right amount to make a good drink, who knows? It's probably because it just looked cool.

Battle-Ready Booze

Alcohol and gunpowder were the lifeblood of a ship and, as such, they were treated with special care, stored together in the safest part of the ship under lock and key. The lock and key were to prevent the alcohol from being consumed all at once and the gunpowder from being used during alcohol-fueled mutinies.

This posed a problem: If any liquor leaked onto the gunpowder, the guns wouldn't fire. But the officers couldn't function *without* their liquor, that would be too cruel. So the Royal Navy had a gin specially made for its officers that was 100 proof. That way, if any gin got on the gunpowder, it would still explode.

IPA (India Pale Ale)

As the British empire encircled the globe, it ran into a rather sticky wicket. It had gotten too big for its beer.

British soldiers and merchants posted abroad yearned for a decent pint, but before the age of refrigeration, that wasn't possible. Especially in India. Beer couldn't be brewed there because of the country's hot weather. And the heat and constant rocking of a five-month ship journey ruined beer sent from England.

India became the Holy Grail of beer markets. A source of great riches, but completely unobtainable. Brewers tried cracking the problem, but on top of their shipping difficulties, there were official tasters in India who refused entry to any beer that didn't quench their thirst properly. And the traditional sweet, dark beer did *not* go down well in the hot weather.

The person who finally cracked it was George Hodgson. In the 1790s, he took a pale ale he'd developed (which was already more suitable as a hot weather refreshment) and he increased the hops and alcohol content, making it much more durable. Exports to India shot up so fast that this new style of beer became known as India Pale Ale.

The empire finally had a beer that could match its global thirst.

Modern Word Origins

BINGE: As in "binge drinking." Derives from the naval phrase "binge the cask," a practice wherein sailors would pour water into an empty rum barrel and slosh it around in hopes of extracting any last drops lurking in the wood.

GROGGY: While it now means tired or punchy, "groggy" originally referred to someone who was drunk on grog. Grog, also known as "three-water rum," was the rather unpopular invention of British admiral Edward Vernon, nicknamed "Old Grog" by his men for his habit of wearing a shabby coat made from grogram, a coarse fabric. In 1740, Vernon ordered the watering down of the navy's superstrong rum, so as to discourage overintoxication.

LIMEY: Vernon also ordered this daily ration of grog to be served with lime juice. Doctors had discovered that scurvy, the mouth rot that plagued sailors for centuries, was easily avoided with regular doses of vitamin C. Vernon was the first to institute the policy of carrying stocks of limes onboard. By the 1880s, this policy had earned British sailors the nickname "lime-juicers" and "limeys" by U.S. and Aussie sailors. "Limey" soon became a general term of derision for all British people. (Incidentally, Admiral Vernon didn't just inspire "groggy" and "limey," he's also the reason George Washington named his estate Mount Vernon.)

SCUTTLEBUTT: This phrase, meaning "gossip or rumor," started where most gossip does—around the water cooler, or at least a nineteenth-century ship's version of a water cooler. A "scuttle" was a lidded opening or hatchway in the deck of a ship and a "butt" was a large cask for holding water, wine, or beer. Sailors in need of a break could dip a cup into this opening and get a drink from the barrel. And like office break rooms and bars everywhere, when people congregate to drink, they'll start swapping the latest gossip. This became the "scuttlebutt news," which was soon shortened to "scuttlebutt."

THREE SHEETS TO THE WIND: In old sailor-ese, a "sheet" is actually a rope. More specifically, one that tied down the bottom corner of a sail and trimmed it to the wind. For those of you not up on your yachting-speak (like me), that means that if the sheets were loose, the sail would rip free and the ship would veer out of control like a drunken sailor careening through the streets. As for the number three, there's no significance, except that three loose sheets is worse than one, the way three drunken sailors are worse than one. The phrase first appeared in print in 1821, so it's probably much older.

On the Three Abiding Traditions of the British Navy

"Rum, Sodomy, and the Lash."
—THE SOURCE OF THIS INFAMOUS QUOTE IS ANONYMOUS, ALTHOUGH IT'S BEEN WIDELY MISATTRIBUTED TO WINSTON CHURCHILL. CHURCHILL HIMSELF MAINTAINED THAT HE NEVER SAID IT, BUT THAT IT WAS SO GOOD HE REALLY WISHED HE HAD.

On Reasons for the Supremacy of British Forces

"Ye true honest Britons who love your land
Whose sires were so brave, so victorious, so free,
Who always beat France when they took her in hand—
Come join honest Britons in chorus with me.

Let us sing our own treasures, Old England's good cheer,
The profits and pleasures of stout British beer;
Your wine-tippling, dram-sipping fellows retreat,
But your beer-drinking Britons can never be beat.

The French with the vineyards are meagre and pale,
They drink of their squeezings of half-ripened fruit;
But we, who have hop yards to mellow our ale,
Are rosy and plump, and have freedom to boot."
       —EIGHTEENTH-CENTURY BRITISH FIGHT SONG

Sir Winston Churchill

(1874–1965)

Are you ready?

Take a deep breath because during the course of his life, Sir Winston Churchill graduated from the Royal Military Academy (England's West Point), was stationed in colonial India, wartime Cuba, engaged in the English military's last cavalry charge, fought in hand-to-hand combat against the dervishes of Sudan, worked as journalist/soldier in South Africa during the Boer War, was captured, sent to a POW camp, escaped in dramatic fashion, and returned to the front to fight, all while reporting on his exploits, earning him worldwide fame that he parlayed into a political career as a Conservative, switched to the Liberal Party, sponsored radical new legislation such as old-age pensions, a minimum wage, and unemployment/health insurance, married, had four children, commanded the British navy during World War I, created the Royal Air Force, oversaw the disastrous landing at Gallipoli, was fired, signed up to fight on the front line, was recalled, oversaw the establishment of the Arab states and an independent Ireland, switched back to the Conservative Party, popularized the phrase "blood, toil, tears and sweat," which he pledged to England when he became prime minister during its "darkest hour," as it stood alone against Nazi Germany, forged the long-standing Anglo-American alliance that brought America into the war and defeated Hitler, was voted out of office two months after the end of World War II, whereupon he declared, "History shall be my judge, and I will write the history," backed this up by winning the Nobel Prize for Literature in 1953 for his nineteen books and dozens of volumes of compiled speeches, was knighted, reelected prime minister at the age of seventy-seven, created the phrase "iron curtain," helped found NATO, displayed his paintings in the Royal Academy, retired, and then, justifiably feeling that he'd accomplished enough in one lifetime, died in 1965.

But what he was *really* known for was drinking.

Before he was even born his mom invented the Manhattan (page 156), and by the end of his life he was chewing through a bottle of brandy a day. But he never made any secret of his hobby. During the Nazi blitz that devastated England, Churchill claimed he survived on "cigars, brandy and crisis."

Here are the numbers:

Tonnage of Nazi bombs dropped on London: 18,800
Civilian deaths in London alone: 30,000
Amount per month Churchill spent on wine, spirits, and cigars:
  Six-month period before the blitz: £183
  Six-month period during the blitz: £421
  Difference: An increase of 230 percent

And his prodigious intake, coupled with his prodigious wit, resulted in some of the greatest aphorisms ever.

"I am easily satisfied with the best."
—ON CHAMPAGNE

LADY ASTOR: Sir, you're drunk!
WINSTON CHURCHILL: Yes, and you, Madam, are ugly. But in the morning I shall be sober.

"Remember, gentlemen, it's not just France we are fighting for, it's champagne!"
—A RALLYING SPEECH DURING WORLD WAR I

"During the war I consumed German wine but I excused myself that I was not drinking it, but interning it."

"In the South African War, the water was not fit to drink. To make it palatable we had to add whisky. By diligent effort I learned to like it."

"Most people hate the taste of beer—to begin with. It is, however, a prejudice that many people have been able to overcome."

"When I was younger, I made it a rule never to take strong drink before lunch, and now it is my rule never to do so before breakfast."

"Well, dinner would have been splendid . . . if the wine had been as cold as the soup, the beef as rare as the service, the brandy as old as the fish, and the maid as willing as the Duchess."
—AFTER ATTENDING A SOCIAL FUNCTION

"In victory we deserve it, in defeat we need it."
—ON CHAMPAGNE

Finally, when he was criticized for hitting the sauce just a bit too hard, Churchill simply replied, "Always remember that I have taken more out of alcohol than alcohol has taken out of me."

EARLY AMERICA:
ONE NATION UNDER
THE INFLUENCE

"Lincoln, Lincoln,
whatcha thinking,
I've a hunch that you've been drinking.
Was it water? Was it wine?
Oh my god it's turpentine!"
—**CHILDREN'S SKIP-ROPE VERSE**

America inherited many of its traits at birth, when the first white settlers came from England and brought the English culture with them: the language, values, and love of drinking . . . a lot (see "every other chapter in this book with the possible exception of sake"). Alcohol was omnipresent in early American life, valued as much for its communal properties as for its inebriating effects. A free barrel of beer was often used as enticement to gather a community together to clear a field or build a town church.

Along with the church, the tavern became one of the vital institutions of any town. It would double as a hospital, jailhouse, or town hall when necessary and was usually run by the town's most upright citizen or the church deacon. Given its central role in the community, as America grew from a handful of settlers into cities and states, a law was passed requiring every town to have a tavern.

So it's no real surprise that from the first foot set on Plymouth Rock to the founding of a free and independent nation, alcohol played a part every step along the way.

Last Call at Plymouth Rock

*"Drink is in itself a good creature of God, and to be received with thankfulness, but the abuse of drink is from Satan, the wine is from God, but the Drunkard is from the Devil." —*INCREASE MATHER, PILGRIM

The *Mayflower* was a rental. Normally used to transport wine between Spain and England, the Puritan Pilgrims hired it to transport them to the New World in 1621. Unfortunately, the Pilgrims were totally unprepared. They were a church group, not well-trained survivalists. They didn't even pack enough beer to make it across the Atlantic.

Contrary to our idea of the word "puritan" now, the Puritans back then weren't abstainers. In fact, during the journey, they "sadly bewailed being deprived of their beer when the supply failed," according to the *Mayflower*'s log. The crew took pity on their passengers and gave them beer from the ship's supply.

But as the *Mayflower* sailed down the eastern coast of America looking for a suitable place to go ashore, the crew realized that sailing any farther would risk their beer supplies running out on the return trip to England. The crew abruptly ran out of pity. They gave the Pilgrims the heave-ho at the next available stop, which is what we now know as Plymouth Rock.

One Pilgrim, William Bradford, recorded the scene in his diary: "[We] were hasted ashore and made to drink water, that the seamen might have the more beer." Bradford then pleads for beer, to which a sailor on the *Mayflower* responds that even if Bradford "were their own father, he should have none."

> "BY MAKING THIS WINE VINE KNOWN TO THE PUBLIC, I HAVE RENDERED MY COUNTRY AS GREAT A SERVICE AS IF I HAD ENABLED IT TO PAY BACK THE NATIONAL DEBT."
>
> —THOMAS JEFFERSON

Stranded in this foreign land without beer, the Pilgrims adapted as best they could, learning to make beer out of pumpkins, turnips, and assorted other things you don't really want to make beer out of. Ultimately, they were reduced to drinking *water*, if you can imagine. Lesson learned.

In 1630, another boatload of Puritans set sail from England on the *Arabella*, and this time they did it right. They traveled with three times as much beer as water, and ten *thousand* gallons of wine, not to mention each Pilgrim's personal stash of distilled spirits.

The call of the New World was answered.

New York State of Mind

In 1609, the Dutch explorer Henry Hudson sailed his ship, the *Half Moon*, to America. Upon landing on an island along the east coast, he encountered members of the Delaware Indian tribe. To foster good relations, Hudson gave the tribal chief some brandy. The chief passed out. But upon waking the next day, he asked Hudson to pour some for the whole tribe.

From then on, the Indians referred to the island as Manahachtanienk. Literally "The High Island." And not "high" in the sense of "tall," but in the sense of "the place where we got blotto." Many would argue that Manhattan has stayed true to the spirit of its name ever since.

Critical Decision

"What event is more awfully important to an English colony than the erection of its first brewhouse?"
—REVEREND SIDNEY SMITH

1587   Virginia colony established. Colonists try brewing their own ale.

1607   Virginia colonists receive first shipment of ale made by real brewers in England.

1609   American "Help Wanted" advertisements appear in London seeking brewers for the Virginia Colony.

Founding Father Facts

- George Washington wore wooden dentures that he would soak in port overnight. It helped numb his gums and provided that slow, smooooth release you need to found a country.

- Thomas Jefferson wrote the first draft of the Declaration of Independence in a Philadelphia tavern.

- Washington, Benjamin Franklin, and Thomas Jefferson all made their own beers and whiskey. Jefferson, in particular, felt that it was the duty of every patriot to become independent of Britain through self-reliance (beer included).

- George Washington at one point became one of America's largest whiskey distillers.

■ Two days before completing the U.S. Constitution, the fifty-five delegates decided to blow off some steam by throwing a party for themselves. According to the tavern bill, they polished off fifty-four bottles of Madeira, sixty bottles of claret, eight bottles of whiskey, twenty-two bottles of port, eight bottles of hard cider, twelve beers, and seven bowls of alcohol punch large enough that "ducks could swim in them."

Ben Franklin's Shadow

When the Founding Fathers gathered in 1787 for the Constitutional Convention, the proceedings were held in secret to prevent rabble-rousing newspapers or potential mobs from interfering while they formulated the U.S. Constitution.

The only real threat to security was Ben Franklin and his fondness for working-class taverns. Ben was famous for turning into a blabbermouth after a few drinks, and the heads of the convention were worried he'd spill the beans. So during the five months they took to write the Constitution, a bodyguard was assigned to follow him into bars and, if he got overly gabby, to drag him out again.

"WINE MAKES DAILY LIVING EASIER, LESS HURRIED, WITH FEWER TENSIONS AND MORE TOLERANCE."

—BENJAMIN FRANKLIN

The Boston Tea After-Party

To protest oppressive British taxation, a party of men rowed out into Boston Harbor dressed as Indians. They intended to board a ship carrying British products and dump its contents overboard. They did so. But what seems to have gotten lost in history is the fact that there were *two* British merchant ships in the harbor that day, and they boarded both.

The first ship carried tea. The tea went into the harbor. The second ship carried hard cider. The cider did not go into the harbor. The raiding party decided to lodge its protest in a less dramatic, but equally patriotic manner—they took the cider home and drank it.

The DWI That Roused a Nation

Paul Revere's famous ride didn't start as a full-throated, wake-the-villages sort of trip. Originally, according to historian Charles Taussig, Revere was simply riding from Charlestown to Lexington to warn Sam Adams (the beer guy) and John Hancock (the big signature guy), two leaders of the Revolution.

But it so happened that his ride took him through Medford, the rum capital of colonial America. Revere stopped for a brief rest at the house of Isaac Hall, the leader of the local Minutemen and distiller of Captain Hall's Old Medford Rum. By the time he saddled up again, Revere had sampled several drams of Captain Hall's hospitality and "He who came a silent horseman, departed a virile and vociferous crusader, with a cry of defiance and not of fear."

It was Revere's drunken caterwauling that roused the Minutemen near Bunker Hill, who got good and drunk in preparation to meet the British head-on, resulting in the first gunfight of the Revolutionary War.

The National Anthem

After witnessing the British assault on Fort McHenry in 1814, Francis Scott Key was inspired to write the lyrics to the "Star-Spangled Banner." He didn't write the music, though, he swiped it from a popular British drinking song, "To Anacreon in Heaven."

This song was written and performed frequently by the Anacreontic Society, an eighteenth-century gentlemen's club in London dedicated to "wit, harmony, and the god of wine." They took their name from the ancient Greek poet Anacreon, whose lyrics celebrated wine, women, and song. The society carried on this tradition with gusto at its concerts/parties, where "the greatest levity, and vulgar obscenity, generally prevailed."

> "IT HAS LONG BEEN RECOGNIZED THAT THE PROBLEMS WITH ALCOHOL RELATE NOT TO THE USE OF A BAD THING, BUT TO THE ABUSE OF A GOOD THING." —ABRAHAM LINCOLN

Johnny Appleseed

John Chapman, better known as Johnny Appleseed, is famous for wandering through the wilderness of eighteenth-century America, planting apple orchards. The children's book version of the story portrays him as a sort of protohippie, planting trees for their foliage and beautiful blossoms.

In reality, apples at the time were used for one reason and one reason only—to make hard cider. As the frontier pushed west, Johnny Appleseed would get ahead of it and plant an orchard so that by the time settlers reached that spot, the apples would be ready to be turned into cider. He died a wealthy man.

Six American Firsts

1. The first federal income tax was placed on whiskey (see "Bourbon," page 88).

2. The first federal consumer protection law was passed to protect the quality of bourbon (see "Bourbon," page 93).

3. In 1614, in the Dutch colony of New Amsterdam (now known as Manhattan), Jean Vigne became the first white person to be born in New York City (then the Dutch colony of New Amsterdam). The birth took place in Block & Christiansen's, America's first brewery. Jean Vigne grew up to be a brewer.

4. The first labor strike occurred in Boston in the 1640s, when the town fathers tried to increase productivity (i.e., decrease worker drunkenness) by outlawing the payment of wages in liquor. Workers went on strike and the town fathers relented.

5. The first paved road was built outside a brewery on Stone Street in New York City. Rain and runoff from the brewery kept turning the dirt road into impassable mud. This caused the terrible prospect of beer wagons being delayed from making their appointed rounds.

6. In 1775, the first Marine Corps recruiting station was established in Tun Tavern, a bar in Philadelphia. The commander in charge of recruiting the men just happened to be the proprietor of . . . Tun Tavern. The bar is even depicted on the insignia ring worn by Marine Corps alumni.

   By coincidence (or *was* it . . .) the Tun Tavern was also used as the first meeting hall for America's first order of Freemasons. Conspiracy nuts, start your engines. . . .

AMERICAN PROHIBITION

"Young men start takin' nips and totin' flasks to be smart and show they're regular fellas. They often show up behind bars or in the gutter without friends or a future. . . . [As for women], often they end up as social outcasts, unmarried mothers, gangster molls, and pistol-packin' mamas." —REVEREND SAM MORRIS, THE VOICE OF TEMPERANCE, FROM HIS FAMOUS RADIO SERMON "THE RAVAGES OF RUM"

"I was a tee-totaller until Prohibition." —GROUCHO MARX

In 50 B.C., King Barebista of Thrace (modern-day Romania) enacted the first Prohibition by banning the use of alcohol in his country. He was stabbed to death six years later. That's a pretty good encapsulation of prohibition's effectiveness through the ages.

In hindsight, Prohibition in America is one of the most famous disasters of legislation in U.S. history, but the Temperance Movement that produced it, while shrill and pious, had a point. Before radios, movies, or television, booze was the entertainment. Nineteenth-century Americans drank an extraordinary, and depressing, amount.

One victim was Carry Nation, who endured a brief marriage to an abusive alcoholic in the late 1800s. By 1900, she was no longer married, but burning with an understandable hatred for alcohol when, one day, while browsing through a hardware store, she came across a hatchet. She was transformed into a holy warrior, a self-described "bulldog running along at the feet of Jesus, barking at what he doesn't like."

She launched upon a campaign of "hatchetations," in which she would march into a saloon and smash it apart. At six feet tall, 180 pounds, she was so imposing that she famously sent John Sullivan, the heavyweight boxing champion of the world, running for his life out the back door of one bar she attacked. She was never an official part of the Temperance Movement, but she gave it star power as her fame spread. Saloons would board up their windows when she came into town.

Before then, the Temperance Movement had been a fairly ineffectual group, despite having millions of members. Groups of women would pray in front of a saloon in hopes of closing it by divine force. Some closed for the day out of sheer embarrassment, but others "baptized" the women by throwing buckets of beer at them.

With Carry's charismatic rallying cry of "Smash, ladies, smash!," temperance gained momentum. Roving bands of women descended on apple orchards that produced hard cider and chopped them down. A new Bible was even issued in which every reference to drinking or wine (over three hundred) had been edited out. Finally, a constitutional Amendment (the eighteenth) banning the production or sale of alcohol made its way onto the floor of Congress. It sailed through with surprising ease.

Ironically, many members of the Temperance Movement thought beer and wine were perfectly acceptable. These were the drinks of stable citizens. They only wanted a ban on spirits, the rum and whiskey their husbands came home stinking of. But then World War I came along, and the wave of anti-German hysteria that swept America picked beer up in its swell, making every six-pack look like the Krauts' fifth column.

Prohibition on all alcohol began at 12:01 A.M. on January 16, 1920.

The Punchline: Four years after Carry Nation's death, a large moonshine operation was discovered on her father's farm in Missouri.

America Meets the Gangsters

Prohibition had the immediate and deleterious effect of turning every law-abiding but imbibing American into a criminal. Drinking became a very, very lucrative criminal activity, and nobody does criminal activity better than organized crime.

The roles of society were instantly reversed—cops became bad guys and bootleggers became heroes. The seamy underbelly of America stepped into the light and the nation got its first good look at colorful if deadly characters like Al "Scarface" Capone, Gertrude "Cleopatra of the Rum-Runners" Lythgoe, and the notoriously violent outfit that patrolled the Great Lakes, the Purple Gang.

The economics were easy enough: a consignment of rum from the West Indies that cost $170,000 could be stepped on until its street value was $2 million. In just one year, Al Capone made $60 million (about $2 billion today).

America's walk on the wild side during Prohibition affected the English language as well. It was as if the entire country went to see a Scorsese movie and came out talking like a wise guy. People became familiar with terms like *gangster, the mob, trigger man, big shot, hot* (stolen), *racketeer, moll, racket, getaway car, taken for a ride, rumrunner, bootlegger, scofflaw,* and *the real McCoy* (for some of these origins see "Glossary," page 259). The word *hijack* supposedly derives from the com-

mand to raise the hands in the air ("Up high, jack!")
given by gangsters who intercepted rogue rumrunners.

G-Men Get the Shaft

Prohibition was rendered utterly toothless right from
the start. Officials estimated that it would take $250 to
$300 million to enforce the law. Congress appropri-
ated a whopping $5 million.

Thus, to patrol the nineteen-thousand-mile border
between Canada and the United States (the world's
longest), there were only 1,520 agents, or one for
every twelve miles. In 1924 alone, it's estimated that
150,000 cases of liquor crossed the Canadian border.

And that was just imports. In 1921, agents seized
95,933 home-brewing stills, but that didn't even slow
things down. In 1930, agents seized—are you ready?—
282,122 stills.

Juries weren't real sympathetic to the government's efforts either. In 1921, out of 1,422 cases that
went to trial *only eighteen of them brought convictions!*

A Brief Guide to Breaking the Law

"Mother's in the kitchen washing out the jugs,
Sister's in the pantry bottling the suds,
Father's in the cellar mixing up the hops,
Johnny's on the front porch watching for the cops."
—A POPULAR PROHIBITION SONG

■ There were several loopholes in the Eighteenth
Amendment. One was for doctors, who were allowed to fill one hundred prescriptions for medicinal whiskey in a three-month period. In
1927, 1.8 million gallons of medicinal whiskey
were ordered. That number rose even higher
the next year, when a record number of doctors

"lost" their prescription pads and ordered re-placements, earning them an estimated $40 million in one year.

- Wine for use during religious services was also legal. America discovered religion (and that loophole) in 1923 when it chugged 2.9 million gallons of ecclesiastical wine.

- At first, Prohibition did serious damage to the American wine industry, as their only option was to sell bottled grape juice. But wine makers soon realized that it was perfectly legal to stick a very large, very prominent label on their bottles that said: "Warning: will ferment and turn into wine." The label would then go on to detail step by step what the customer should avoid doing if they want to prevent grape juice from turning into demon wine.

- Housewives and many members of the Temperance Movement swore by the healing powers of the "revitalizing tonics" that came into fashion, most of which contained around 40 percent alcohol.

- The Bacardi Rum company found itself stuck with sixty thousand cases of rum in its warehouses when Prohibition hit. So they formed a side company in which they sold sixty thousand shares. They then declared the company was kaput, and distributed its assets to the tune of one case of rum per shareholder.

- If a rumrunner's boat was overtaken by the Coast Guard, he would put his contraband whiskey in a sack attached to a large block of salt and heave it into the ocean before getting boarded. When the Coast Guard's search turned up nothing, they were forced to let him go, and he would come back to the spot eight to ten hours later, when the salt dissolved and the whiskey bottles would come floating back to the surface.

■ One London gin company received an order from America for a very large consignment of gin, cash in advance. The one stipulation was that the consignment had to be packaged in such a way that it could float.

Speakeasy

The term "speakeasy" to describe an illegal drinking establishment was first used at the end of the nineteenth century. It derived from the need to speak softly and strictly hush-hush about its existence.

What the women of the Temperance Movement couldn't have predicted was that the rise of these illegal clubs gave a real boost to women's lib. Speakeasies were democratic places—if your money was green, you could drink. Up until then, bars had been the domain of men. No women allowed. But now, men could take their wives out for a nightcap or to see a show. And in response to their first public dose of liquor, music, and dancing, women's hemlines rose and the Jazz Age was kicked into high gear by the flashing gams of flappers, America's first party girls.

Pre-Prohibition, New York City had fifteen thousand legal saloons. By the end of Prohibition, it had over thirty thousand illegal ones. Boston seemed quieter, racking up only four thousand speakeasies, until you realize that that was four times more than were in the entire state of Massachusetts before Prohibition.

Drinks

Smuggling real liquor couldn't keep up with the speakeasies' demand, so bootleggers began making bathtub liquor with names like Yak Yak Bourbon, Old

Horsey, Happy Sally, Soda Pop Moon, Jersey Lightning, and Squirrel Whiskey (so named because one sip would make you dig your nails into the bark of a tree and race up it).

These noxious concoctions were simply rubbing alcohol cut with glycerine, iodine, or anything else that improved the taste. Needless to say, it didn't improve the taste very well, so people had to mix their liquor with fruit juice and, in the process, invent the cocktail (see "Cocktail").

When improperly made, these bootlegged liquors caused blindness, paralysis, or death (see "The Final Score," below).

The End

Prohibition lasted thirteen years, ten months, nineteen days, seventeen hours, thirty-two minutes, and thirty seconds.

It was put out of its misery on December 5, 1933, at 6:55 P.M., with the ratification of the Twenty-first Amendment. Upon signing it, President Franklin D. Roosevelt—clearly the greatest president ever—declared, "I believe this would be a good time for a beer."

The Final Score

- Estimated number of people killed, blinded, or paralyzed from bad liquor: 50,000.

- Number of innocent bystanders killed in shootouts between police and rumrunners: over 1,000.

- Population of federal penitentiary system before Prohibition: 4,000. After Prohibition: 26,000.

- Acreage of California devoted to wine before Prohibition: less than 100,000. After Prohibition: 700,000.
  (The U.S. government probably didn't help Prohibition's cause in 1929 when it loaned money to Californian wine makers to help them expand their farmland.)

- Effect of Prohibition on national alcohol consumption: an *increase* of 11.6 percent.

Ten Odd Laws and Outdated Regulations

- King Henry VIII created regulations for the officers of his bedchambers stating that if they were to "cause the maids of the king's household to become mothers [they] will go without beer for a month."

- The UK is the only country that designates a minimum age for drinking at home—five years old, but only with parental consent.

- Texas state law prohibits taking more than three sips of beer at a time while standing.

- In Fairbanks, Alaska, it's illegal to feed a moose an alcoholic beverage.

- Ohio state law prohibits getting a fish drunk.

- Nebraska state law prohibits bars from selling beer unless they are simultaneously brewing a kettle of soup.

- In Saskatchewan, Canada, it's illegal to drink water in a beer parlor.

- It's illegal to sit on any street curb in St. Louis, Missouri, and drink beer from a bucket.

- No alcoholic beverages can be displayed within five feet of a cash register of any store in California that sells both alcohol and motor fuel.

- State law of North Dakota prohibits serving beer and pretzels at the same time in any bar or restaurant.

MISCELLANEOUS GREAT MOMENTS IN WORLD HIC-STORY

Drink Like an Egyptian

- The first toothpaste was a mixture of wine and coarse pumice dust, created by the Egyptians about five thousand years ago. This was a good deal better than the toothpaste created by the Romans that lasted until the eighteenth century. Its chief ingredient was urine.

- Pharaohs were often buried with tiny model breweries (including wooden brewer dolls) to ensure they would have plenty of beer on the journey to the afterlife.

- The ancient Egyptians believed that . . .

   . . . you could cure love sickness by drinking beer out of an old shoe.

. . . drinking a mixture of beer foam and chopped onion would ward off death.

. . . intoxication was next to godliness. So they gave their children names such as "How Drunk Is Cheops" or "How Intoxicated Is Hathor" (see "Hathor," pages 193).

The Origins of Honeymoon

Four thousand years ago in Babylonia, a bride's father would give his son-in-law all the mead he could drink for a certain amount of time following the wedding. Mead is a honey beer, and since the Babylonian calendar was lunar, this period was called the "honey month." Today, it's called a "honeymoon."

The First Drinking Game

Kattabos: A game invented by the Greeks in which the dregs of a cup of wine would be thrown at a metal disk held in the hand of a statue. The player who knocked the disk off won. Like most drinking games, it sounds asinine but it proved popular enough to last over three hundred years after its birth in 600 B.C.

The First Breathalyzer

The custom of a woman being greeted with an embrace by her family or friends is thought to have begun with the early Romans. Only it wasn't intended as a pleasantry, it was to smell the woman's breath for traces of wine. Wine was strictly forbidden to women, as its consumption led very quickly to acts of adultery.

Merry Olde England

- In medieval England, there were very few local courthouses, so judges would travel to towns and marketplaces and set up court in the one building that was sure to be present—a tavern.

- In the eighteenth century, a gentlemen's dinner party consisted of eight hours of solid drinking and eating. On such occasions, one servant's sole task would be to loosen the necktie of anyone who passed out so as to prevent them from choking. Urine pots would be located in sideboard drawers so men wouldn't have to stumble all the way to the bathroom.

- Part of a workman's wages were paid in beer. When Ben Franklin went to England in 1765, he gave an exact account of the drinking habits at the printing shop he visited: every worker had one pint before breakfast, one pint with breakfast, a pint between breakfast and lunch, a pint at lunch, a pint at six o'clock, and a pint at the end of the working day. The average allowance of beer to workers in the eighteenth century was a gallon a day.

- The 1915 Defense of the Realm Act closed English pubs in the afternoon hours between lunch and five o'clock. It was thought that the war effort was being hindered by factory workers who went to the pub for lunch, then didn't bother going back to work.

Prussian Pick-Me-Up

When coffee was introduced into Prussia, Frederick the Great tried to ban it. He declared in his 1777 edict: "It is disgusting to notice the increase in the quantity of coffee used by my subjects, and the amount of money that goes out of the country as a consequence. Everybody is using coffee; this must be prevented. My people must drink beer. His Majesty was brought up on beer, and so were both his ancestors and officers. Many battles have been fought and won by soldiers nourished on beer, and the King does not believe that coffee-drinking soldiers can be relied upon to endure hardships in case of another war."

Oktoberfest

Lederhosen, oompah bands, and fat guys stirring vats of sauerkraut with pitchforks, for sixteen days in September (ironically) Munich's Oktoberfest is the beeringest place on earth. The festival started in October 1810, when Crown Prince Ludwig of Bavaria held a giant horse race to celebrate his marriage to Princess Therese of Saxony. The festival was unusual because the prince opened the festival to the general public even though royalty almost never mingled with the commoners. Forty thousand people attended the first Oktoberfest, and the event was such a hit that they decided to hold the festival every year in the same meadow.

Ironically, beer only started being served in 1818, but being German, the festival-goers took to it with such vigor that the horse racing soon went out the window. And every year after, the festival grew bigger and beerier until its fame spread worldwide.

Today, about 6 million people attend and, in 2002, they oompahed their way through 5,761,400 liters of beer and, surprisingly enough, 1,004,000 liters of non-alcoholic beer. They topped it off with 219,405 pairs of sausages, 58,746 pork knuckles, and 87 oxen.

The Rum Rebellion

The only successful (though temporary) military takeover of the Australian government was the Rum Rebellion of 1808.

In its early days, the Australian economy had a problem. There wasn't enough money (actual physical bills and coins) to even *have* an economy. So the colonists began using rum as a form of currency.

This only created further problems. For starters, it was an inefficient currency, as it tended to get consumed before it could be used again. Secondly, the sugarcane needed to make the rum was grown on land owned by officers in the New South Wales Corps, the British regiment sent to establish order in the colonies. So the NSWC effectively owned rum, which meant they controlled the entire economy, and acted accordingly, running roughshod over any governor who tried to oppose them.

Enter the sadistic Captain William Bligh, the same Captain Bligh of *Mutiny on the Bounty* fame, someone who just couldn't seem to stop pissing people off. Bligh tried to ban the use of rum as currency. The NSWC took exception to this and to his tyrannical style of governing and held a military coup. Bligh was held under house arrest for over a year until England sent a new governor to replace him. The NSWC was then disbanded, and beer and wine consumption encouraged.

Words of Advice

Any time we try a new beer, a new wine, a new liquor, brand, or cocktail, we're like mad scientists in old movies, willingly turning our bodies into chemistry sets in order to monitor the results. Not only how it tastes, but how it feels. Did that drink turn you into Jekyll, or was it Hyde? Which combination of drinks made you warm and witty and which made you vomit in your friend's glove compartment?

This experiment has been performed nightly for centuries by everyone from the greatest artists and philosophers to teenagers in the woods behind their house. And, over the years, they've come up with some pretty specific conclusions. So it would be wise to stop at this juncture and ponder the advice that has filtered down through the ages:

"Liquor before beer, never fear. Beer before liquor, never sicker." —AMERICAN COLLEGE STUDENT PROVERB

"Beer before wine, you'll feel fine. Wine before beer, you'll feel queer." —ENGLISH PROVERB

"Cider smiles in your face, and then cuts your throat."—OLD ENGLISH PROVERB

"Boys should abstain from all use of wine until their eighteenth year, for it is wrong to add fire to fire."
—PLATO, GREEK PHILOSOPHER AND NOTED CONNOISSEUR OF EIGHTEEN-YEAR-OLD BOYS

"Take counsel in wine, but resolve afterwards in water." —BEN FRANKLIN

"Always do sober what you said you'd do drunk. That will teach you to keep your mouth shut."
—ERNEST HEMINGWAY

"1 martini is alright, 2 is too many, 3 is not enough."
—JAMES THURBER

The "rule of three" as seen in the quote above has been a maxim that's run throughout history. In the Talmud, one drink turns you into a lamb, two a lion, three a pig, and four an ape. The idea that "three drinks is the tipping point" is in everything from the Bible to ancient Greek poetry to European folklore (see "The Many Stages of Drinking," page 247). In fact, as the shape and size of the wine bottle has evolved over the centuries, it's taken this into account. The modern wine bottle is designed for two people to have three drinks each.

ONE TOO MANY

> *"What'll you have?"*
> *"One too many."*
> —AL COHN, JAZZ MUSICIAN

If you've reached this point, it means you've ignored the Words of Advice on the previous page. You've ignored the little person in your brain telling you to call it a night. You've gone past your limit; one drink too far; one toke over the line. But before you know where to draw the line, you have to step over it a few times.

When you do, it can prove to be a pleasant experience or a painful one, but whichever way it goes, there's no turning back because, buddy, for the next few hours, you're drunk.

"Drunk"

There are more synonyms and slang expressions for the state of being drunk than any other word in the English language. When compiling his first *Poor Richard's Almanac* in 1732, Ben Franklin noted 228 alternate wordings. Slang dictionaries in modern times recognize over 1,000. The only things that even come close to having that many slang expressions are the various naughty bits located around the human body.

"THE INN-KEEPER LOVES THE DRUNK-ARD, BUT NOT FOR A SON-IN-LAW."
—JEWISH PROVERB

When Breathing Was Better

The Breathalyzer was patented in the early 1950s. Unfortunately, it was efficient enough to phase out the original 1930s breath-analysis machine, the fantastically named Drunkometer.

Beer Goggles

An experiment by the Psychology Department at Glasgow University discovered that after a person has consumed four units of alcohol (about two pints of beer or half a bottle of wine), their perception of the attractiveness of members of the opposite sex increases by 25 percent. Or as Jackie Gleason noted, "Drinking removes warts and wrinkles from women I look at." (For further descriptions of this effect, see "On the Perils of Alcohol and Ugly Women," page 101).

Pink Elephant

This mythic creature has become a universal symbol of what people see after drinking too much. In films, the appearance of the elephant prompts the drunkard to do a double take, rub his eyes in disbelief, look at the elephant again, then glare at his bottle accusingly before throwing it into a garbage can.

The concept first appeared in print in the 1890s, only it was a pink *giraffe* galloping in and out of the drunkard's vision. It officially transformed into a pink elephant in 1913, when Jack London wrote, "There are, broadly speaking, two types of drinkers. There is the man whom we all know . . . who . . . falls frequently in the gutter, and who sees, in the extremity of his ecstasy, blue mice and pink elephants."

It has given rise to the slogan: "Pink elephants are a beast of bourbon."

The Spins

Your body's sense of balance is provided by your inner ear in which there's a small blob of jelly, known as a cupola, that acts as your brain's gyroscope. When you're drunk, you get dehydrated, which alters the shape and size of the cupola, prompting your brain to think your body is spinning around. The direction the room spins is determined by which side you rest your head (and thus your inner ear) on.

The reason the spinning gets worse when you close your eyes is that you're shutting off the visual input your brain uses to tell itself that your ear is wrong.

Four Tricks of the Trade

- Sipping your drink through a straw increases the ratio of your intake of alcohol to oxygen, which makes the alcohol travel to your brain faster. Or you could just tie a plastic bag over your head for a few minutes.

- A strong drink is absorbed more slowly by your body than an average one. The valve that leads into your stomach actually closes from shock when it's hit with a shot of high-proof spirits, and then only lets it leak in slowly, whereas beer or wine passes straight into your stomach and bloodstream.

- Using a carbonated mixer may dilute a drink, but it actually speeds up your body's digestion of the alcohol. Experiments with champagne have shown that bubbles can increase your body's absorption rate by as much as 70 percent.

- "Boot and rally": While this phrase most likely originates with American teenage boys and college students, the technique of purging your stomach to make room for more alcohol was pioneered by the Romans, who built vomitoriums for this express purpose.

> "Don't you know alcohol kills brain cells . . . any damn brain cell that can't live through a good drunk deserves to die. You're doing yourself a favor, getting rid of all them nonhacking, underachieving ones. I'm working on improving your efficiency."—JAMES WEBB, A COUNTRY SUCH AS THIS

God-Forgive-Me

The name for a large two-handed drinking vessel used in parts of England during the eighteenth and nineteenth centuries, presumably named because of the contrition felt the next morning by the person who drank the whole thing.

Four Dumb Deaths of Four Famous Men

- Fifth century: Attila the Hun, the unstoppable leader of half a million bloodthirsty barbarians, scourge of the steppes, scourge of the Roman empire, nicknamed the Scourge of God, and someone who just generally did a lot of scourging, finally met his end on his wedding night. After a night of heavy drinking, it is believed that he stumbled unnoticed from his tent, fell over and broke his nose before he went to bed and passed out. He died in his sleep from suffocating on his own blood.

- During a drinking contest with a rival, Alexander the Great drank twelve *pints* of wine. His rival matched him, so Alexander called for twelve more pints, which he tried to chug in one go. He died, thus losing the contest.

- Tycho Brahe, a sixteenth-century Danish astronomer whose pioneering work led to Newton's discovery of gravity, died after attending a dinner party with the Baron of Rosenberg. Tycho consumed a great deal of wine during the course of the meal; however, leaving a host's table to pee was considered a major breach of etiquette at the time, so Tycho crossed his legs and continued drinking. Unfortunately, his bladder didn't share his sense of decorum; it burst and he died a slow and painful death eleven days later.

- Sherwood Anderson, the writer of *Winesburg, Ohio*, put a novel twist on the concept of drinking yourself to death. In 1941, he attended a cocktail party at which he managed to stab himself in the gums with the toothpick in his martini. He set sail the next day on an ocean liner bound for Brazil, but he never made it. An infection set into his gums and he died of peritonitis en route.

> "BUT I'M NOT SO THINK AS YOU DRUNK I AM." –SIR JOHN SQUIRE

Some Sobering Statistics

- Alcohol consumption is involved in two-thirds of all homicides, and three-quarters of all non-fatal stabbings.

- Men are four times more likely than women to drive while drunk.

- Accident-proneness increases 50 percent when the blood alcohol level goes from .01 to .05. It doubles again from 0.05 to 0.06, and quadruples at 0.08. At .15, you're twenty-five times more likely to be involved in an accident.

- 24 percent of alcoholics die in accidents, falls, fires, and suicides.

- Between the hours of 10:00 P.M. and 4:00 A.M., 75 percent of all pedestrians killed by traffic are over the limit.

- Alcohol is the fourth-leading cause of death in the U.S. and UK.

> "DEBAUCHEE, N. ONE WHO HAS SO EARNESTLY PURSUED PLEASURE THAT HE HAS HAD THE MISFORTUNE TO OVERTAKE IT." –AMBROSE BIERCE

- In Eastern Europe and Russia, alcohol is the cause in one out of every three deaths!

- People who die from one night of binge drinking average twenty drinks in under two hours.

The Many Stages of Drinking

"The first glass contains health. It has a healing power, an herb, within it. Pick it and it will grow.

"Take the second glass. In that is hidden a little bird that sings an innocent song, and man listens to it and agrees: Life is Beautiful! Let us not be downhearted, but live!

"The third glass contains a little winged child, half angel, half pixy. He does not tease maliciously but is filled with fun. He climbs into our ears and whispers amusing thoughts and warms our hearts so that we feel young and gay and become witty and amusing, even according to the judgment of our friends at the party.

"The fourth glass has only an exclamation point in it, or maybe a question mark. This is the point which sense and intelligence never go beyond.

> "AN ALCOHOLIC IS SOMEONE YOU DON'T LIKE WHO DRINKS AS MUCH AS YOU DO."
>
> —DYLAN THOMAS

"After you have drunk the fifth glass, then you either weep over yourself or you become sentimental. Prince Carnival jumps from the glass and draws you into a dance, and you forget your own dignity; that is, if you ever had any. You forget more than you should, more than it is good for you to forget. All is song, music, and noise. The masked ones whirl you along; the

Devil's daughters in silk dresses, with their long hair and their beautiful legs, join the dance. And you, can you tear yourself away?

"In the sixth glass sits the Devil himself; he is a little well-dressed man, most charming and pleasant. He understands you and agrees with everything you say. He even brings a lamp to light your way—not to your home, but to his. There is an old legend about a saint who was ordered to experience one of the seven deadly sins. He decided that drunkenness was the least of them. But as soon as he got drunk, then he committed the other six sins. In the sixth glass the Devil and man mix blood; in that thrives everything evil within us, and it grows like the grain of mustard in the Bible until it becomes a tree so large that it shades our whole world. Then we are fit for nothing but to be melted down again." —HANS CHRISTIAN ANDERSEN, *THE WATCHMAN OF THE TOWER*

"I HAVE NEVER BEEN DRUNK, BUT I'VE OFTEN BEEN OVER-SERVED."
—GEORGE GOBEL

"AN INTELLIGENT MAN IS SOMETIMES FORCED TO BE DRUNK TO SPEND TIME WITH HIS FOOLS."—ERNEST HEMINGWAY

THE HANGOVER

"The wrath of grapes" —JEFFREY BERNARD

Every New Year's Eve, newspapers trot out the same articles about hangovers—how they happen, how to avoid them, how to cure them. And every New Year's Day, it's all for naught. Hangovers are like bad weather, sometimes they just happen. There's nothing that can be said about them that most people haven't figured out by their sophomore year of college.

But for the record, hangovers are caused by loss of vitamins B and C, salt, and various minerals. But mainly, it's dehydration. It's estimated that for every pint of alcohol consumed, the body loses one and one-quarter pints of water.

The only 100 percent foolproof method to avoid them is abstinence. But, like celibacy, that probably ain't gonna happen. So you know the basic routine. Don't drink on an empty stomach. Take an aspirin and lots of water before going to bed. And most importantly, don't mix your drinks.

A general rule of thumb is, the lighter the drink, the less the hangover. Vodka, gin, and white wine have fewer impurities than dark drinks like whiskey, brandy, and red wine. If you're looking to blame anyone or anything other than yourself for your condition, you can blame the impurities (known as "congeners"). They're the actual cause of the throbbin' in your noggin.

> *"I will never mix gin, beer, and whiskey again."*
> —PULITZER PRIZE–WINNING JOURNALIST WESTBROOK PEGLER, IN A FAMOUS NEW YEAR'S DAY COLUMN THAT CONSISTED ENTIRELY OF THIS PHRASE REPEATED OVER AND OVER AGAIN FIFTY TIMES

THE SUFFERING

It's a Small (Excruciating) World After All

In America, we call it a hangover (starting around 1904), but just as alcohol is a universal language, so is the pain its overuse produces. Every culture has come up with its own description of this wretched state. Below are some literal translations of foreign expressions for a hangover.

SPAIN: A nail in the head; the pounding of waves on rocks; the ooze.

GERMANY/NETHERLANDS: The wailing of cats.

FRANCE: Wooden face.

SWEDEN: A pain in the root of the hairs.

NORWAY: Carpenters in my head.

ITALY: Out of tune.

CUBA: A gnawing in the stomach.

PORTUGAL: Kill the beast.

MYANMAR: Clapper of the temple bell.

FINLAND: The Finnish word for hangover is *krapula*. This is self-explanatory.

SOUTH AFRICA: In Afrikaans, it's *vrot*, which means "gone rotten, like an apple." But South Africans also refer to a hangover somewhat fondly as a "Barbie," from the Zulu word for hangover, *babalas*.

Veisalgia

For those of you interested, this is the actual medical term for a hangover. It's a conflation of the Norwegian word *kveis*, meaning "uneasiness following debauchery," and the Greek word *algia*, meaning "pain." Although why they bothered coining this fancy term is unclear, since the medical definition admits that "there is no consensus definition of veisalgia." It's when you just sort of feel, you know . . . hung over.

The All-Time Greatest Description of a Hangover

"Consciousness was upon him before he could get out of the way. . . . The light did him harm, but not as much as looking at things did; he resolved, having done it once, never to move his eyeballs again. A dusty thudding in his head made the scene before him beat like a pulse. His mouth had been used as a latrine by some small creature of the night, and then as its mausoleum. During the night, too, he'd somehow been on a cross-country run and then been expertly beaten up by the secret police. He felt bad." —KINGSLEY AMIS, *LUCKY JIM*

The First Hangover?

In the Egyptian religion, Shesmu was the god of wine and the winepress. And like wine, he could be friendly . . . or vengeful. In a papyrus from the Twenty-first Dynasty, two of his henchmen are shown crushing human heads instead of grapes in a winepress.

NORA: WHAT HIT ME?
NICK: THAT LAST MARTINI.
—*The Thin Man*, 1934

Double Suffering

Hangovers can hurt your wallet as well as your head. Between employees calling in sick and decreased productivity from the ones who *do* manage to stumble into work, hangovers are estimated to cost the United States economy about $148 billion every year. The UK, despite its binge-drinking habits, only lose about $4 billion a year. But no one can beat the Finnish, who, with a population of just 5 million people, manage to miss over 1 million days of work a year due to hangovers.

THE CURE

In general, greasy food, lots of water, and some fruit juice with vitamin C helps. But there *is* no real cure except to resign yourself to your fate and wait it out.

Hangover Hokum

Where science fails, folk remedies and old wives' tales always move in to pick up the slack. Here are thirteen surefire cures conjured up over the centuries and around the globe:

PUERTO RICO: Rub half a lemon in the armpit of your drinking arm.

JAPAN: Wear a gauze surgical mask soaked in sake.

MONGOLIA: Eat/drink pickled sheep's eye in tomato juice.

HUNGARIAN MAGYARS: Drink sparrow droppings in brandy.

ANCIENT ASSYRIANS: Grind swallow beaks into myrrh and drink.

ANCIENT LIBYANS: Mix seawater into your wine. That way, you can't get too much wine into your system before the seawater induces vomiting.

ANCIENT GREEKS: Draw blood through self-flagellation, allowing the alcohol to seep out.

ROMANS: Eat a fried canary.

MIDDLE AGES: Drink a mixture of bitter almonds and raw eel.

WILD WEST: "Plenty of droppings from a jack rabbit," well dried, then brewed with hot water in a tea.

NINETEENTH-CENTURY AMERICAN HOUSE-WIVES: *Miss Theo P. Winning's Household Manual,* a medical bible for the lady of the house, suggests soaking your feet in mustard and water until the headache disappears.

NINETEENTH-CENTURY ENGLISH CHIMNEY SWEEPS: A cup of warm milk mixed with a teaspoon of soot (from hardwood, if possible), drink slowly.

HAITI: The voodoo cure—stick thirteen black-headed pins into the cork of the bottle that caused the hangover.

Eggs Benedict

Invented in 1894 by Lemuel Benedict, a guest at the Waldorf-Astoria Hotel. The desperately hung over Benedict stumbled down to brunch and ordered his own personal remedy—poached eggs over ham on buttered toast topped with hollandaise sauce. The maître d' immediately recognized this dish as the Holy Grail for hangover sufferers. He put it on the Waldorf menu and named it in Mr. Benedict's honor.

DESPERATE MEASURES

All right, admittedly, there is *one* cure—have another drink, a pick-me-up, a brain-duster, an eye-opener. But even if you can manage to get a drink down (and *hold* it down, that's the important part), all you're doing is putting the pain on hold for a while. It'll come back sooner or later. But sometimes you've gotta do what you've gotta do . . .

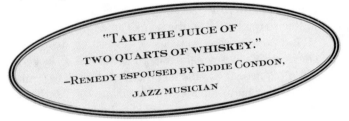

"TAKE THE JUICE OF TWO QUARTS OF WHISKEY."

–REMEDY ESPOUSED BY EDDIE CONDON, JAZZ MUSICIAN

Hair of the Dog

This phrase first appeared in English in 1546. It originally referred to the medieval belief that a dog bite could be cured if a few hairs from the dog were laid across the wound. This cure was soon phased out on the grounds that it was idiotic, but its name carried on as a useful metaphor for drinking.

Bloody Mary

The pinnacle of hangover perfection. If you're going to bite the bullet and order a drink, this has got the spice to wake you up, the tomato juice to soothe your stomach, and the vodka to ease the pain.

The Bloody Mary was invented in 1921, by Fernand "Pete the Frog" Petiot, the bartender at Harry's New York Bar in Paris, the famous hot spot for American ex-pats. It was a cutting-edge drink at the time, since it was made with vodka, a novelty drink that had just been introduced into France following the 1917 Russian Revolution (see "Vodka," page 130).

Some people claim that a customer (who obviously had some issues) told Pete the drink reminded him of the Bucket of Blood Club in Chicago and his ex-girlfriend, who worked there, Mary. Others claim the drink was named in tribute to the silent film star Mary Pickford. Either way, the Bloody Mary was a hit, and when Pete moved to the King Cole Bar at New York's St. Regis Hotel in 1934, the drink came with him.

But New Yorkers were more discerning drinkers. The King Cole regulars told Pete his drink lacked oomph. Maybe it was the fact that Pete had to use gin, since vodka hadn't made it to the States yet. Maybe it was the name—the owner of the St. Regis thought the word "bloody" was undignified; he demanded it be called Red Snapper. So Pete began oomphing it up with black pepper, Tabasco, and horseradish, and by the time vodka became available and the Red Snapper name died a quick death, the Bloody Mary was back and better than ever.

As for the celery stick, it apparently came into being in the 1960s during a party at the Ambassador East Hotel in Chicago. As Bloody Marys were passed around, the bar ran out of swizzle sticks, so one swizzleless socialite simply replaced it with a piece of celery she took from a passing tray. The hotel maître d' noticed and made it a standard garnish.

I'll Never Drink Again

Before AA, alcohol addiction was neither well understood nor well treated. In the 1920s, doctors treated drunks by switching their addiction from alcohol to morphine. And several centuries before that, according to British historian J. D. Rolleston, the Russian cure consisted of "taking a piece of pork, putting it secretly in a Jew's bed for nine days, and then giving it to the drunkard in a pulverized form, who will turn away from drinking as a Jew would from pork."

That changed in 1935, after a chance meeting between Bill Wilson and Dr. Robert Smith, or, as they became better known, Bill W. and Dr. Bob.

Born in 1895, Bill W. became a Wall Street stockbroker and full-fledged alcoholic by his early twenties. He got sober by following a six-step program developed by a religious organization known as the Oxford Group. But during an unsuccessful business trip to Akron, Ohio, Bill wanted a drink, and decided that only a fellow recovering alcoholic would understand him enough to help (which later became Step 12—take your experiences and use them to help fellow alcoholics).

He located Dr. Bob, who had been an on-again, off-again alcoholic since his days at Dartmouth University, and together they made it through the night. They began treating other alcoholics in Dr. Bob's home, expanding the six steps and making them more accessible by dropping the Christian references for a more general "higher power." In 1939, they published *Alcoholics Anonymous,* which went on to sell millions of copies. AA is now in 150 countries with over 2 million members worldwide, all of which begins with a single step: "We admitted we were powerless over alcohol—that our lives had become unmanageable."

- **A Friend of Bill:** A phrase sometimes used by people in Alcoholics Anonymous to describe themselves.

- **Dr. Bob's Nightmare:** The phrase used in AA books preceding any personal account of an alcoholic's life.

- The country with the highest number of AA groups per capita is Iceland, with one group for every 1,250 people.

A GLOSSARY OF INEBRIATED ENGLISH WORDS AND PHRASES

BALDERDASH: A dismissive term to describe something as nonsense or rubbish. The English phrase originally meant "a jumble of words," but it came from Scandinavia as a dismissive term for "a mixture," referring to a poorly mixed, weak drink. In England, it came to mean a combination of drinks that didn't mix well, such as beer and wine or beer and milk.

BARMY: This British term for someone who's crazy comes from the word "barm," which is the froth that builds up on top of beer when yeast is fermenting. *Barmy* implied that someone had froth or bubbles for brains.

BLIND TIGER/BLIND PIG: Mid-nineteenth-century American slang for illegal drinking establishments that cropped up in areas where it was illegal to sell individual drinks, or sometimes when bar owners simply didn't want to pay for a license. They would advertise animal curiosities like those found in a carnival sideshow, and anyone who wanted to step right up and see the blind tiger or blind pig could pay an entrance fee to go into the bar—where they would receive a "complimentary drink."

BLOODY: This British expletive started cropping up in literature in the late seventeenth century in the phrase "bloody drunk." It was similar to another expression, "drunk as a lord," and referred to a generation of young aristocrats who were becoming a public nuisance due to their excessive drinking and subsequent asinine behavior. The "blood" referred to their aristocratic bloodline, or their position as true blue bloods (which interestingly enough is a relatively racist term that started among purebred aristocratic Spanish families who believed that their blood was blue as opposed to the commoners, whose blood was black from mingling with the African Moors).

BOOTLEG: Originated in the American West in 1855. It was illegal to sell liquor to Indians (blacks, too), so traders would hide small bottles of whiskey inside their boots in order to smuggle it to them.

BOOZE: There are several options for this word's origins: *Bouzah* was the name of an ancient Egyptian beer. *Buizen* means "to drink to excess" in Dutch. And *bauschen* is German for "to swell or inflate." The final possibility is that it derives from the name of a popular nineteenth-century Philadelphia distiller, Mr. E. G. Booze.

BUMPER: As in a "bumper crop," a crop that has produced to its full capacity. Dating from 1759, a "bumper" was originally a glass that was filled to the brim for a toast (thus forming a bump of liquid over the rim of the glass).

CODSWALLOP: This old-fashioned British term for "nonsense" is a bit of a word origin mystery. But one of the more popular theories is that it refers to Hiram Codd, a soft-drink manufacturer in nineteenth-century England. Fizzy soft drinks weren't possible until bottles were developed that could keep the fizz in. Hiram became one of the first to solve the problem by inventing a bottle that had a glass marble stuck in the neck, trapping in the carbonation. To open the drink, you just had to push the marble down into the bottle. Unfortunately, his bottle also looked like beer bottles at the time. So when his line of Codd's lemonade hit the market, people looking to buy beer were outraged to find that, by mistake, they'd bought a drink utterly without alcohol. A popular slang term for beer was "wallop," so "codswallop" came to refer to anything that was worthless or pointless.

FIASCO: A debacle or humiliating failure. Came into English in 1855 as theater slang for an actor who flops on stage. But it originated from the Italian word for bottle, *fiasco* (which is also the origin for our word "flask"). The best explanation for the connection between "failure" and "a bottle" is that it comes from the phrase *fare il fiasco*, which several centuries before meant "to play a game so that the one that loses will pay the *fiasco*." In other words, to mess up was a costly mistake because the loser buys the next round.

HOBNOB: The origins of this word date far back into Old English, when the phrase first meant "to have or have not." By Shakespeare's time, it had mutated into meaning "a give and take." And if this sounds like a good description of two people drinking and talking, that's exactly what it came to mean in the eighteenth century—the socializing that goes on in pubs. "To drink a hob nob" meant to exchange toasts with each other. It's only in the last hundred years or so that hobnob has dropped its association with pub life and come to mean any form of friendly interaction.

HOOCH: This slang for illegal liquor started with the Hoochinoo Indians in Alaska, who distilled liquor and sold it to appreciative miners during the Klondike gold rush. *Hoochinoo* became a shorthand word for liquor in 1869, and by 1890, it had been shortened to the now-familiar "hooch."

JITTERBUG: In the nineteenth century, a good deal of the liquor sold was of such terrible quality that drinking it might give you the "jitters," an uncontrollable shaking. A "jitterbug" was the term for someone who drank excessively, and, in 1934, Cab Calloway, with a good dash of gallows humor, turned it into a song and dance craze.

MIND YOUR P'S AND Q'S: In old England, a bartender would mark a customer's tab up on a chalkboard as he ordered pints or quarts of beer. If a customer was getting too drunk, or seemed to be overspending his limit, the bartender would remind him to check his tab on the chalkboard or "mind his p's and q's."

MUG: Originally, a mug was simply a drinking vessel for beer. But in the eighteenth century, they were frequently decorated with a grotesque human face, and "mug" became slang for someone's face. The way "mug" is used in 1930s gangster movies (to describe a patsy or a dunce) came from the idea that you could pour anything into a mug.

ON THE WAGON: Originally "on the water wagon," this term for someone who doesn't drink alcohol started over a hundred years ago, before roads were paved. A wagon carrying a tank of water would travel around towns spraying the roads to prevent dust from rising. The phrase probably arose simply because the wagon was one of the more recognizable symbols for water.

PACK MY BOX WITH FIVE DOZEN LIQUOR JUGS: This phrase—used by typesetters—has been sadly forgotten over the years. Its claim to fame is that it's the one other sentence in the English language, along with "The quick brown fox jumps over the lazy dog," that uses every letter in the alphabet.

POP GOES THE WEASEL: This phrase, now known for its use in the children's rhyme, is actually based on a popular song (and dance) from Victorian London. One of the original verses was:

> *"Up and down the City Road,*
> *In and out the Eagle,*
> *That's the way the money goes,*
> *Pop goes the weasel."*

The Eagle was a pub at the time. "Pop" was slang for pawning and the "weasel" was Cockney slang for a coat. The other verses are a catalogue of ways in which the city chips away at the paychecks of the working-class poor and forces them into hock.

THE REAL McCOY: There are many theories as to who inspired this phrase, but one of the main contenders is Jim McCoy, a Prohibition bootlegger. It was said that his bathtub liquor imitated brand-name liquors so well that they became known as "the real McCoy."

RULE OF THUMB: Beer has to be just the right temperature for yeast to work, and before the advent of thermometers, brewers would stick their thumb into the vat to gauge the heat. A "rule of thumb" became a term for a general estimation or guideline.

SCOFFLAW: During Prohibition, so many people flaunted the antidrinking laws that the police wanted to create a new word for "criminal" that would strike fear into the hearts of would-be drinkers. So, in 1924, a multimillionaire named Delcevare King sponsored a contest to create a new name. For a prize of $200, 25,000 entries were received, and "scofflaw" was the winning entrant.

SKID ROW: The place you end up when you've drunk yourself into bumhood. The term comes from logging camps in the American West, where workers would slide logs down a track they called a "skid road." They soon applied the name half-jokingly to the collection of brothels and whiskey tents that sprang up to meet the needs of the loggers. It was thought of as a place where men of weak constitutions could quickly slide out of society altogether. Visiting easterners misheard the name as "skid row" and brought it back to the cities.

TUMBLER: The name of this glass stems from a Saxon toasting custom in which you had to down your drink in one go. To ensure that you couldn't cheat, a vessel was created with a rounded bottom that couldn't be put down without tumbling over and spilling out any leftover liquid. Nowadays, the bottom is flat but the name remains.

WET YOUR WHISTLE: Ceramic drinking mugs in England would sometimes have a whistle welded onto the rim. The whistle came in handy when looking for a refill. Instead of trying to catch the bartender's eye, the customer could simply give a tweet on his mug.

FOR THE BEST IN PAPERBACKS, LOOK FOR THE

In every corner of the world, on every subject under the sun, Penguin represents quality and variety—the very best in publishing today.

For complete information about books available from Penguin—including Penguin Classics, Penguin Compass, and Puffins—and how to order them, write to us at the appropriate address below. Please note that for copyright reasons the selection of books varies from country to country.

In the United States: Please write to *Penguin Group (USA), P.O. Box 12289 Dept. B, Newark, New Jersey 07101-5289* or call 1-800-788-6262.

In the United Kingdom: Please write to *Dept. EP, Penguin Books Ltd, Bath Road, Harmondsworth, West Drayton, Middlesex UB7 0DA.*

In Canada: Please write to *Penguin Books Canada Ltd, 90 Eglinton Avenue East, Suite 700, Toronto, Ontario M4P 2Y3.*

In Australia: Please write to *Penguin Books Australia Ltd, P.O. Box 257, Ringwood, Victoria 3134.*

In New Zealand: Please write to *Penguin Books (NZ) Ltd, Private Bag 102902, North Shore Mail Centre, Auckland 10.*

In India: Please write to *Penguin Books India Pvt Ltd, 11 Panchsheel Shopping Centre, Panchsheel Park, New Delhi 110 017.*

In the Netherlands: Please write to *Penguin Books Netherlands bv, Postbus 3507, NL-1001 AH Amsterdam.*

In Germany: Please write to *Penguin Books Deutschland GmbH, Metzlerstrasse 26, 60594 Frankfurt am Main.*

In Spain: Please write to *Penguin Books S.A., Bravo Murillo 19, 1° B, 28015 Madrid.*

In Italy: Please write to *Penguin Italia s.r.l., Via Benedetto Croce 2, 20094 Corsico, Milano.*

In France: Please write to *Penguin France, Le Carré Wilson, 62 rue Benjamin Baillaud, 31500 Toulouse.*

In Japan: Please write to *Penguin Books Japan Ltd, Kaneko Building, 2-3-25 Koraku, Bunkyo-Ku, Tokyo 112.*

In South Africa: Please write to *Penguin Books South Africa (Pty) Ltd, Private Bag X14, Parkview, 2122 Johannesburg.*